HOW TO: USE INNOVATION IN THE WORKPLACE

Patrick Collister was the executive creative director of Ogilvy & Mather, which was fun. Then creative director of a large direct marketing agency, which was not. Perhaps the best fun ever was when he led the creative team in northern and central Europe for a global media owner.

In between times, he has founded several businesses: Creative Matters is a training consultancy offering programmes and workshops to help businesses use creativity and innovation to good effect, *Directory* is a magazine devoted to innovations in communications and 'The Big Won Rankings' is an annual report on the leading agencies and campaigns around the world as measured by the quantity and quality of awards won.

He has a wife called Dorte, which can be confusing, and they live with three dogs in a half-built barn in Kent.

how to: ACADEMY launched in September 2013. Since then it has organized over 400 talks and seminars on Business, Lifestyle, and Science & Technology, which have been attended by 40,000 people. The aim of the series is to anticipate the needs of the reader by providing clarity, precision and know-how in an increasingly complex world.

PATRICK COLLISTER

HOW TO: USE INNOVATION AND CREATIVITY IN THE WORKPLACE

bluebird
books for life

First published 2017 by Bluebird
an imprint of Pan Macmillan
20 New Wharf Road, London N1 9RR
Associated companies throughout the world
www.panmacmillan.com

ISBN 978-1-5098-1445-9

9 8 7 6 5 4 3 2 1

A CIP catalogue record for this book is available from the British Library.

Printed and bound by CPI Group (UK) Ltd, Croydon, CR0 4YY

Visit **www.panmacmillan.com** to read more about all our books
and to buy them. You will also find features, author interviews and
news of any author events, and you can sign up for e-newsletters
so that you're always first to hear about our new releases.

Contents

INTRODUCTION

In many ways, this is an almost impossible book to write.

If you want to know how to repair a gasket leak to the intake manifold of a car, that's easy. There's even a YouTube video to show you how to do it. There are step-by-step guides in books and in online video tutorials detailing how to make chutney, how to put together an IKEA dresser and, alarmingly, even how to make a real gun that shoots real bullets. But how to have an idea? They just pop into your head, don't they?

John Cleese has told audiences that he is often asked where he gets his ideas from.

He says he gets them from Ken Livenshaw, who lives in Swindon. He, in turn, gets his ideas from Mildred Spong, who lives on the Isle of Wight.[1] As he explains, no one really knows where ideas come from or why having ideas is so hard. What we do know is that new ideas are the fuel for change.

When an idea is turned into an artefact, when you can make a prototype, then what you have on your hands is sometimes an invention but more probably it is an innovation.

It all starts with an idea.

As a species, *Homo sapiens* is unique in having the imagination to be able to project both backwards and forwards in time. We can discuss with each other things that don't exist. Yet. That's what an idea is – it's a projection forward, in which you can envisage people using, enjoying and benefiting from what you have made. It could be a book or a painting, or it could be a new low-energy lightbulb or a novel way of containing rat populations. Be you writer or painter, designer or biologist, however, you occupy a field of endeavour which, further on, I have called a 'creative domain'.

The domain is usually your specialist subject. The more knowledge and understanding you have of the subject, the greater the likelihood that you will be able to have ideas and to innovate. And that's where, perhaps, this book can help.

Ideas come to the prepared mind. You can't predict when the synapses of the brain suddenly snap, crackle and pop but when they do, it can be breathtaking.

This, then, is more than anything a manual on how to prepare your mind. Where possible I have tried to use stories as well as instruction, because following someone else's example is sometimes easier than following a blueprint.

In my past I was the creative director of a large ad agency. I remember suggesting to a senior copywriter that he might learn a thing or two by going off to a training workshop. He didn't fancy it. 'Nah. Either you can effin' do it or you can't,' he told me.

Actually, he was wrong. The brain is like a muscle – the more it gets used, the more agile it becomes. Similarly, the most inventive people I know are constantly open to new stimulation.

In the following pages, you will find plenty of suggestions to help you flex that muscle. If this book helps prompt just one idea that proves to be worthwhile, even as a stepping stone to another, bolder idea, then the last few months sitting at my desk while the dogs have moaned gently about all the missed walks will have been worth it.

1:

DEFINING CREATIVITY

What is creativity?

Well, if you are a Christian, then it all starts at the beginning, when, according to Genesis, Chapter 1, Verse 1, 'God created the heaven and the earth. And the earth was without form, and void; and darkness was upon the face of the deep.'

According to the Koran, Allah created the earth and the heavens in six days.

So, there's one answer to the question: creativity is about making things. Literally, creating.

However, if you are a Hindu, then creativity is about endless worlds coming into existence and then disappearing. The Lord Brahma created the world; the Lord Vishnu preserved it only for the Lord Shiva to destroy it.

Creativity in this context, then, is a story of never-ending innovation.

Buddhists, on the other hand, believe that there is no reason to imagine the world had any sort of beginning at all. In which case, creativity is the art of making do with what is in front of you.

Putting various deities aside, creativity is an innate human characteristic. Just about every human being is creative in that he/she can make things. Make a cake, make a table and, when we work collaboratively, even make a rocket and send it to the moon.

We share 99.4 per cent of our genes with chimpanzees and yet this morning, you pulled back your sheets of woven cotton, printed with dyes made by a panoply of chemicals, and got out of a bed constructed from tempered steel, plastics and wood from a forest a thousand miles away. You may have made a cup of coffee relying on the electricity you can control at the flick of a switch, with beans flown here from Ecuador, before the internal combustion engine helped get you to your office.

Most chimps woke up in a tree, wondering where the next banana was going to come from.

The huge difference between us and our primate cousins is we have thumbs and they don't. They have five fingers. They can pick things up but they do not have the manual dexterity we have.

Man is a manipulator.

Turning this page, for instance, is a delicate task beyond most apes.

Creativity, then, is an evolutionary quirk which occurred some three million years ago, when one of our australopithecine ancestors developed opposing thumbs.

Sharp thinking

Lucy, aka *Australopithecus afarensis*, was a runty little creature. She already stood on two legs to survey the savannah around her in that part of Africa which today straddles Kenya and Ethiopia. But her thumbs gave her an astonishing advantage. She could make things.

She was able to pick up a couple of stones and bang them

together in such a way that one of them developed a sharp cutting edge.

Her descendants learned to flake stones in a manner that enabled them to make hand axes.

They used these to crush, scrape, cut and flay.

They became butchers of animals.

Intriguingly, there is some evidence that the use of hand tools led to further evolution of the hand. It became stronger as its uses became more varied and more important for survival.

Lucy was making things with a point. In other words, when she picked up the stones to bang them together, she had an idea of what she wanted to do and why she wanted to do it.

One of her descendants was *Homo habilis*, the tool-maker. Like Lucy, he was discovered at Olduvai Gorge in Tanzania. He was surrounded by thousands of tools.

He had created an entire technology around stone-banging.

At first he seems to have used his axe to smash the bones of animals to get to the marrow inside.

But then he made what the boffins call a cognitive leap.

He thought, *What if I use one stone, the hammerstone, to strike a second stone, the core, at an angle? If I get it at the right angle on exactly the right spot, I can flake off a thinner, sharper piece.*

He invented the hand axe and soon afterwards he invented the knife.

He was having ideas and testing those ideas made him an innovator.

This flint is sharp. Now, what else can I do with sharp?

I wonder if I can project sharpness?

What happens if I tie this sharp point to a thin stick? Now I have a spear.

And what happens if I stretch this piece of gut from tip to tip of this other bigger stick?

Oh, look! A bow and arrow.

I can kill small animals.

I can flay the animals' skins and scrape them and cure them then cut them and make myself a natty little tunic.

Sharp also means I can cut branches, I can cut them to length, I can make a shelter. I can build a village.

Over the next half a million years, a nanosecond in terms of evolution, the human brain doubled in size. *Homo habilis* had a larger brain than Lucy, arguably because he was asking more questions.

Questions we are still asking.

What does sharp mean? It means lasers that slice through metal, or diamond wire cutters that saw stones into perfect blocks. It even means inter-continental ballistic missiles.

The early history of mankind is an astonishing catalogue of discovery and invention.

It seems likely that hominids, all the man-like creatures that pre-date *Homo sapiens*, were using fire 500,000 years ago. Fire already existed but discovering how to control it, that was a huge leap. It created the environment in which they could invent cooking. That, in its turn, gave human evolution another massive shove in the small of the back.

Cooked food isn't just more easily digested than raw; it provides as much as 30 per cent more energy. All very useful for the expanding brain.

The wheel, subject of many inaccurate jokes about Stone Age man, wasn't invented for another 495,000 years.

Probably more significant as an idea was agriculture.

Around 30,000 years ago our prehistoric ancestors were harvesting oats in Italy.

By the Bronze Age they had invented the hoe.

By the Iron Age they were using ploughs.

And building canals to export their products.

And inventing slavery in ancient Egypt in order to be able to farm more intensively as well as to embark on ambitious building projects.

Agriculture was a huge idea. It allowed communities to stay put. They didn't have to wander from place to place, foraging. They could grow their populations. They could stockpile provisions and protect themselves from famine. They could maintain armies.

Of course, agriculture wasn't *an* idea. It was, and still is, a constantly evolving chain of experiments, many of which failed to work.

For instance, as a boy growing up in East Africa, I often passed the desolate remains of the grandiose Tanganyika Groundnut Scheme at Kongwa. (After WWII, the colonial government thought it could ramp up the country's economy by making it the world's largest producer of peanuts. It turned out it couldn't.)

One idea leads to another.

It always has. It still does.

First principle of creativity:
It's about solving problems

Before getting any deeper into what creativity is, let's take a moment to reflect on what it is not.

I often wish there was another word for it, especially in the context of growing business. When I run creative thinking workshops, executives regularly turn up expecting to be made to play with finger paints and connect with their inner selves. They are universally relieved to learn they are not going to be made to behave as six-year-olds again.

Creativity is a word that seems to have been hijacked by the Romantic movement of the eighteenth and nineteenth centuries.

That was when the image of the struggling visionary became popular, the lone voice in the wilderness, the tortured soul.

Even now the creative genius is seen as someone tousle-haired and wide-eyed, at odds with the establishment. A rebel, a black sheep, a person ahead of the times.

This is annoying.

Creative people look very much like you and me.

They are engineers and traders, publishers and coffee shop owners.

They are people who have a vested interest in doing things well.

After all, even if you work for someone else, doesn't it make the job more rewarding to know that you're doing it properly?

People who just go through the motions each day must have horribly desiccated minds.

Creativity is *not* the preserve of the artistic world.

Nor is it to be confused with talent. When I was the creative director of a large ad agency, we had a couple of visualizers in the studio. They could both draw like Raphael. But neither was remotely creative.

People who can draw have a facility, a talent if you like. But that's as far as it goes.

People who can draw but who experiment with the rules of perspective, of line and form, who look to find new ways of making drawing relevant to new audiences, they are creative people.

Picasso galloped through Fauvism and Symbolism, not to mention Surrealism, inventing Cubism along the way as well as the art of collage.

Richard Branson went from a student magazine to a record shop to an airline and a mobile phone company, taking in a train line and a bank along the way.

Creativity, as you can see, can exist in countless different domains.

Painting, sculpture, music – these are creative domains.

But then so too are architecture, advertising and origami.

In 2014, the UK's creative industries grew by 8.9 per cent. They are said to contribute nearly £10 million an hour to the national economy. Chief among them are fashion, computer games and television programmes, all of which we export to the rest of the world. These are relatively new creative domains.

But then civil engineering is a creative domain.

And many bridges are works not just of amazing construction but astonishing beauty.

Car design too. You can't look at an Aston Martin and not be wowed by the lines.

What about pottery? Emma Bridgewater seems to have done pretty well out of her mugs and cups.

So, what constitutes a creative domain?

There seem to be three rules.

1. *You have to agree that whatever it is you're talking about is a creative domain.*

    For example, football.

    When José Mourinho was manager of Real Madrid, was he a creative whizz when, in 2012, he finally worked out how to beat Barcelona?

    Was Zinedine Zidane the creative genius of the midfield when he played for Manchester United in 2015?

    If you are nodding here, then you have just agreed that football is a creative domain.

    What about synchro swimming?

    Ah well, that's altogether more contentious, isn't it? Even though the judges at the Olympics give points for artistic expression.

2. *A creative domain has to have its own literature.*

    So, marketing has *Marketing Week*.

    The wine trade has *Decanter*.

    No prizes for guessing who *Chef Magazine* is aimed at.

    But then there are also titles like *Physics Today*, *Chemistry World* and *Geological Magazine*, which has been in print since 1864.

3. *A creative domain has its own heroes.*

    I know who mine are. Who are yours?

Why is this at all relevant?

Well, if you can bring yourself to see your business as belonging to a creative domain, then you are preparing your mind to challenge its accepted wisdoms and find new ways of doing things.

You are setting yourself up to innovate.

Where creativity is having ideas, innovation is making them happen.

Theodore Levitt described creativity as *thinking up* new things and innovation as *doing* new things.

When it comes to the world of business, and even that of science, innovation is, in many ways, the acceptable face of creativity.

Take the law, for instance. A creative lawyer is almost as dodgy as a creative accountant. But innovation . . . well, that's different. And in fact, even that most august of institutions, the *FT*, has its Innovative Lawyers Awards. And accountants are equally proud of their innovators.[2]

Even organizations that would hate to be creative want to be innovative.

The difference between innovation and invention

Invention is when you come up with something completely new. It is a product or a service that comes into being for the first time.

Innovation is when you apply your mind to the invention to improve it.

I've heard it said that invention is like a pebble thrown into a pond. Someone had to toss the pebble. The inventor. But entrepreneurs watch the ripples and try to turn them into waves.

Inventions are few and far between, and give rise to countless innovations.

By and large, inventions solve problems that people didn't know existed. The car is a good example. As Henry Ford said, 'If I'd given people what they wanted, I'd have given them a faster horse.'

Right now, there are two technological inventions that, together, are altering every single aspect of human life: the computer and the Internet.

Both continue to evolve at incredible speed.

People weren't exactly chomping at the bit for a new way to communicate when Sir Tim Berners-Lee came up with what in 1991 he called the worldwide web. But once he created the world's first website, giving instructions on how others could create websites like it, the genie was out of the bottle.

For entrepreneurs watching the ripples, there has never been a better time to start up a business than now.

There is optimism and money.

Moore's Law[3] may only apply to computing hardware but plenty of investors seem to think there is a doubling of capability and a doubling of value across *all* new technologies.

In their cheery book *Abundance: The Future Is Better Than You Think*, Peter Diamandis and Steven Kotler list the most fertile of new technologies as being:

— Infinite computing – the growth of the cloud
— Sensors and networks
— Robotics
— 3D printing, the 'democratization of distribution'

— Synthetic biology, creating new foods and fuels
— Digital medicine
— Nanomaterials
— Artificial Intelligence

Every one of these areas is fertile terrain for innovation.

Not all new ideas are good ideas

One caveat here: there is an assumption that all new technology must be good technology. That any new development has to be an advancement.

Not always true.

Take the American way of execution.

For most of the nineteenth century, convicted murderers were hanged by the neck on a rope.

Then a Buffalo dentist named Alfred P. Southwick invented the electric chair.

However, it wasn't always as humane a way of ending a life as Alfred may have hoped. There were terrible stories of prisoners being cooked alive.

The technology had been well thought through.

The first jolt was supposed to frazzle the prisoner's brain, rendering him/her unconscious so he or she would be unaware of the second jolt, designed to arrest all the other organs.

It just didn't always work.

As far back as 1903, Fred Van Wormer was executed at Sing Sing prison. When he was taken into the mortuary, he was seen to be still breathing.

By this time the executioner had gone home.

He had to be fetched back to electrocute Van Wormer a second time.

As recently as 1982, when Frank Coppola was executed, his head and leg caught fire.

It was only in 2008 that the Nebraska State Court decreed that execution by electric chair was a 'cruel and unusual punishment'.

By this time, many states had introduced the lethal injection instead.

Chemistry has its own technology and the science of toxins has come on in leaps and bounds in the last half-century so it was assumed that this would be an effective and relatively civilized way of ending a person's life.

Again, not so.

The Death Penalty Information Center reckons that lethal injections have the 'highest rate of botched executions'.[4]

Today, it is worth remembering that a lot of innovations may have novelty value but they will have little more.

Consider the humble app.

There are some amazing apps.

Google Chrome, Facebook, the *Guardian* – these are three on my own mobile which get tapped a lot.

Elsewhere in the App Store, though, there are millions of completely meaningless ideas. One guess is that 80 per cent of all apps have never been downloaded.

For instance, the Chinese Abacus.

Yes, download to your mobile phone an abacus and move coloured beads along a slide to count in exactly the way they did two thousand years ago.

Why would anyone do this, given every smartphone comes with a calculator pre-installed?

How about the Zipper app? It lets you pull a zip up and down. That's it. Although, excitingly, you can customize the colour of the underwear fleetingly revealed in unzip mode.

What were they thinking when they designed the Passion app? And wouldn't we like to know who they were? The app encourages you to turn on the microphone on your iPhone so it can pick up the noises of your lovemaking to give you a score for your sexual performance.

Pursuit of novelty is not the same as looking for an idea that will create value.

In the world of digital communications, I'm often being asked for an idea that is a world first, something that has never been done before.

This is irresponsible creativity.

The true creative has ideas that are useful and usable.

The true creative doesn't just have ideas and pass them on to others to implement. He/she knows that both God and the Devil are in the details.

Henri Poincaré put it nicely over a century ago, when he wrote:

> To create consists precisely in not making useless combinations and in making those which are useful and which are only a small minority. Invention is discernment, choice.
>
> . . . Among chosen combinations, the most fertile will often be those formed of elements drawn from domains which are far apart. Not that I mean as sufficing for invention the bringing together of objects as disparate as possible; most combinations so formed would be entirely sterile. But certain among them, very rare, are the most fruitful of all.

Creativity is a synonym for competitive

So, let's go back to the question again. What is creativity?

If we go back to Lucy, she was only 1.1m (3ft 7in) tall. She had no armour, no tusks and she was not quick on her feet.

She was way down the food chain in a part of the world that specialized in animals that were faster than she was and a lot more ferocious.

Lions and leopards, principally. In the Kruger Park in South Africa, one study estimates that 70 per cent of baboon deaths are at the claws of leopards.[5] Lucy wasn't much bigger than a baboon, remember.

One three-year-old australopithecine called the Taung child appears to have been carried off by an eagle. Its skull shows talon marks in the eye sockets.

Though anthropologists argue about this, it is quite possible early hominids were food for each other.

Yet Lucy survived. In Darwinian terms, she was able to compete successfully. In fact, her descendants have become the most successful species the planet has ever seen.

We have never paused in our competition with other species. We have explored every nook and cranny of the world and pushed their former residents to the margins or to extinction.

Creativity, then, is the instinct to compete and to do more than just survive – to thrive. To get to the top.

Second principle of creativity:
You have to be competitive

Creative people are competitive people.

One of the things I do with my spare time is to monitor advertising awards shows around the world.[6]

Last year, we entered details of some 12,000 totally separate pieces of work, which had won a Gold, Silver or Bronze somewhere.

We probably missed another 12,000.

Globally, advertising awards are a billion-dollar industry.

As well as the big international shows, every country has its own local events, usually with a gala dinner at which the gongs get handed out.

It is competition in the raw.

The huge hurrahs from the agency tables that have won.

The grumpings from the agencies that have not.

Architecture has its competitions too and the art world gives us the Turner Prize every year to provoke us while the Venice Biennale mystifies us every two years.

The 2015 winner of the Biennale Golden Lion was Adrian Piper. The piece for which she received the prize was a request she made to all visitors to the show that they sign a contract with themselves agreeing to always do what they say they will do.

Marvellous.

There are the BAFTAs, the Golden Rose of Montreux, the EMMYs and the daddy of them all, the Oscars.

Creative people like to measure themselves against their peers. Winning prizes confirms their sense of identity as creative.

Awards aren't only handed out within the artistic domains of film, theatre, the plastic arts and advertising.

There are competitive people with the same needs for recognition and reward in all the sciences.

Grandest of all the awards schemes is the Nobel Prize.

Freud once wrote that what drives creative people is the desire for fame, fortune and beautiful lovers.

By and large most Nobel prize-winners tend to be getting on in years and, mostly, a bit beyond the lust-for-lovers stage of life. But in terms of fortune, the prize is worth serious money.

The amount varies each year, depending on how much the Nobel Foundation actually has in its coffers. It has come down from ten million Swedish kroner to eight million. That's a bit above £700,000. Still not to be sniffed at, though Jean-Paul Sartre did sniff at it in 1964.

There are awards for just about every business sector you can think of.

The British Accountancy Awards.

The European Flexographic Industry Association Annual Print Awards.

The Oil & Gas UK Awards.

One of my favourites is Lawyer of the Year. I wonder by which criteria you win that accolade?

The ballroom of the Hyde Park Hilton hosts an awards dinner four or five times a week.

The *Sunday Times* publishes leagues of Best Businesses to Work For.

There is Start-up of the Year.

There are the UK Tech Awards, the National Business Awards, the British Invention Show.

Perhaps the most significant league table of all is the

FTSE 100, or, in the States, the Fortune 100. Every day you can monitor the rise and fall of companies.

Making it into the FTSE 100 is a significant moment, and so too is falling out of it.

Just as life was savage and bloody for our earliest ancestors, so it still is in the Square Mile today. Every market is red in tooth and claw. Every struggle between companies and brands for dominance in their sector is a battle to the death.

If this sounds a little dramatic, consider this: in the sixty years since the Fortune 100 was invented, only 12 per cent of the companies which originally featured in it still remain.

In the UK, over 50 per cent of FTSE 100 companies have gone since 1999.[7]

Every market is a fight to the last.

Take the portable computer.

It evolved into the laptop and then into the tablet and smartphone.

Amstrad, Apricot, Atari, Compaq, Commodore, Sinclair, Tandy, Tiny, Texas – these are all companies that have fallen by the wayside as Apple, Dell, HP, Lenovo and Sony muscled them aside.

Think of the human costs involved when those companies went to the wall. People lost their jobs, many had to move from their homes to find new work; they were industrial refugees. Truly, every market is a battleground.

Hot dogs and a cold calculation

It has become an oft-repeated saw that 'today is the day of least change you will experience in the rest of your lifetime'.

If you are a creative person at heart, you will embrace this truism. You will want to be in charge of change rather than have it happen to you.

Ron Dennis is the CEO of the McLaren Technology Group, part of which is the Formula One team. At the Cannes Lions Festival in June 2014, he said:

> 'I'm brutal. If you don't adapt and change, you die. If you look at our business, it's a very competitive world. A hundred and six teams have come and gone in the time I have been involved in Formula One, which is somewhat over thirty years. These teams get created, there are huge sums of money involved and they fail. They fail because they don't understand the fundamentals of being in a sport that doesn't take prisoners. You have to enter Formula One with the mindset of being competitive. Now, there is a different between competitiveness and competing. When you compete, you are a participant. To be a competitor, you have to adapt and change. Our speed of development is mind-blowing. In season, we are making a new component, designed, developed and manufactured and going onto the car every twelve and a half minutes.'[8]

If you compete, you are simply taking part.

If you are competitive, you don't just hope to win, you plan to win. You *expect* to win because you do everything imaginable and quite a lot that's not to make sure you end up on the podium.

It was his obsession with the minutiae that helped Clive Woodward send out a team that won the Rugby World Cup.

Sir Alex Ferguson's attention to detail was equally remarkable.

Sir Dave Brailsford, British cycling coach, took everything those other great sporting leaders did and turned it into a process. He called it 'the aggregation of marginal gains'.

If you can improve every aspect of the team's performance by just one per cent, overall the one per cents add up to a whacking great advantage.

He looked to do everything one per cent better. The pillows – could they be one per cent better to improve his athletes' sleep by one per cent? The antibacterial hand gel?

He looked for weaknesses in order to turn them into strengths, and British cycling went from being laughable to unbeatable.

Those three guys have each written books about their approach to building teams that win. They're worth reading (see Bibliography, page 189). The one thing the three have in common, though, is a pathological aversion to being beaten.

George Bernard Shaw once wrote, 'The reasonable man adapts himself to the world; the unreasonable one persists in trying to adapt the world to himself.'

To be competitive, you need to start working on an unreasonable mindset.

For example, Takeru Kobayashi has made himself a good living as a champion eater.

In 2001, while still a student, he turned up and won Nathan's Coney Island Hot Dog Eating Contest.

The record stood at twenty-five dogs demolished in twelve minutes.

He doubled it: fifty dogs down.

He wasn't a large fellow by any means. Just 5 foot 8 inches. What he could do, though, was look for marginal gains.

He calculated that breaking a hot dog in half made it easier to chew. Also, it freed his hands for faster loading.

He tested eating hot dogs sprayed with water or with oil.

He put himself on camera so he could watch what he did and develop better ways of 'chesting' and swallowing.

In business, the comparisons with sport make most sense as and when you are invited to submit a competitive bid for a project.

How much or how little do you leave to chance?

When Mercedes-Benz put their advertising account up for pitch, my pal Peter S. led his agency's bid.

He wrote his opening speech. Then filmed it. And re-wrote it. And filmed it again. And won the business.

Afterwards, one of his people said something to him along the lines of, 'Blimey, Pete, that was all a bit OCD, wasn't it?'

To which he answered, 'Well, for eighty million dollars I thought it was worth putting a bit of work in.'

Marginal gains.

The point of being competitive is that you try to do even the tiniest things a little bit better than you think your competition will do them. No improvement is too small.

The Virginia Mason Hospital in Seattle has become a beacon for what can be done in healthcare when you look for marginal gains.

Doctors and nurses were encouraged to be open about mistakes, and this led to changes in labelling on drugs so they could be more easily identified in moments of stress.

Coloured wristbands were attached to patients to help with diagnosis and treatment. But any nurse who was colour-blind could easily get these wrong. So text was added as well as colour. And so on.

The result has been a 74 per cent reduction in the liability premiums the hospital pays its insurers. If you're going to fall ill, try to do it in Seattle. The Virginia Mason is one of the safest hospitals in the world.

Third principle of creativity: You have to work at it

The word 'inspiration' comes from the ancient Greeks.

They believed that while men slept, they might be visited by the gods, who would breathe into them. In-spire them, literally.

Blow their minds, you might say.

They'd wake up fizzing with ideas.

In the Italian Renaissance, Michelangelo's gifts could only be explained as coming from God. He was called *el divino*, the one who was blessed.

So was Raphael.

And Luis de Morales.

Exactly.

There were quite a lot of *el divinos*.

Anyone with exceptional talent was reckoned to have been brushed by divinity.

Today, the Almighty's grip on the collective imagination has been loosened.

From Darwin through to Richard Dawkins and *The God*

Delusion, rational thinkers have pooh-poohed the concept of an all-seeing, all-knowing super-being.

So, how come some people have gifts and others don't?

Mozart had exceptional gifts. But what is sometimes forgotten is that his father was a musician, and so he had music swirling around him from before he was born.

Picasso's father was a painter, and so he was learning about painting before he had learned to talk. By the age of thirteen, it is said Picasso could draw like Raphael. From that moment on, he was exploring new ways of expressing how he felt about the world around him.

Is creativity an accident of birth? Or is it acquired? The answer is both.

In terms of nature, creative people do need to have above-average intelligence. But they don't need to be super-intelligent. They don't have to have Mensa-level IQs. What they do seem to be able to do is live with paradox. They have their feet on the ground but their heads are up in the clouds.

They are rational dreamers.

They are often complex in themselves but search for simplicity.

They enjoy chaos because within it they can find order.

Give them a haystack and they'll love seeing your face when they bring you the needle. They like ambiguity.

The psychologist and writer Mihály Csíkszentmihályi spent decades studying creative people.[9] What he noticed was different about them was that they seemed capable of pursuing a variety of thoughts simultaneously.

Where non-creative people were able to follow only one

line of enquiry at a time, creative people appeared to have multiple rivers of investigation. Creative people are 3D.

Back to Mozart – it seems that musical ability can be identified within a particular cluster of genes.[10] So, Wolfgang Amadeus was the beneficiary of a very particular inheritance. However, without nurture, his creative nature would have shrivelled and died as habit took control of the mind.

'The Minnesota Study of Twins Reared Apart' assessed the creativity of twins who had been raised in different environments.[11] Where one twin was more creative than the other, it was down to the environment in which he/she had been raised. Nurture was fundamental.

If creativity could not be nurtured, then I wouldn't be writing this book. The *Guardian* Masterclasses on writing and publishing, journalism and photography would not be packed out. *Floodlight* would be a much shorter list of evening classes and part-time courses available in London.

Last year alone, over 24,000 people took a City Lit course, in subjects ranging from 360° Photography to Acting for Fun, and from Classical Mythology to Build a Website in a Day. Arguably every single category of course available is a creative domain in its own right – Agriculture, Art & Craft, Beauty, Communication & Media, Cookery, through to Teaching and Writing. You name it and you can do it.

Do you genuinely want to use creativity and innovation to make more of your life? Buy *Floodlight*. Sign up for a course. The more random the better.

Ever since Samuel Smiles published *Self Help* in 1859, Brits have looked to improve themselves through nurturing their interests. Because when an interest becomes a skill, then you have the wherewithal to change your life.

One ex-army officer I know is now a successful wedding photographer. Another ex-army officer is a singer/songwriter. James Blunt went from a tank in Bosnia to *Top of the Pops*.

Slightly more down to earth but equally inspiring is the charity worker who did a course in anatomy and physiology, as well as one in fitness instruction, and now runs her own Pilates centre in the city. She leaped off someone else's career ladder onto her own. She would say she was lucky. Lucky she discovered her vocation, lucky that her teachers saw her potential, lucky that a couple of business angels wanted to invest in her fitness studio.

Actually, luck had nothing to do with it.

As Thomas Edison put it so famously, 'Creativity is 1 per cent inspiration and 99 per cent perspiration.'

Fourth principle of creativity:
You have to accept that you are different

Roger Sperry won the Nobel Prize in 1984 for his work on the brain.

Some of his research sounds as if he was working hand in glove with Nurse Ratched from *One Flew Over the Cuckoo's Nest*.

In himself, Sperry was something of a Renaissance man, in that he saw no obstacles to being both arts-minded and scientifically inclined.

His degree was in English but he became interested in psychology, which led him to study primates. That led him to biology and from there it seemed a natural step to progress to neurology.

He was a serial collector of 'ologies'.

In his private life, he was a dab hand with watercolours and was said to be a talented ceramicist.

In his professional life, at Cal Tech, he started looking at the circuitry of the brain.

He experimented with cats, then people, literally splitting their brains by cutting the *corpus callosum*, the bit between the two hemispheres.

When some unfortunate was reduced to just half a brain, Sperry noticed that the person was still able to function. But their way of thinking was changed.

At its simplest, Sperry suggested that left-brained thinkers were logical, rational, they liked lists, they were analytical and objective.

Right-brained people tended to be more random in their thought patterns, more intuitive. They could see the whole picture more easily.

Today, behavioural psychologists sneer at left-brain/right-brain theory. But not a day goes by when I don't see these two radically different ways of dealing with creative ideas come up against each other.

My old friend Derrick Hass used to infuriate the planners he worked with by leaping to ideas before they were even halfway through briefing him on a task.

Sometimes he leaped to spectacularly inappropriate ideas. (I still remember Floatin' Otis, a hippo who lived in cereal bowls filled with Quaker Oats.)

The very different personalities were captured in the classic movie *The Odd Couple*. Jack Lemon is Felix, fussy, anal, left-brained. Walter Matthau is Oscar, a messy sports journalist who lives in chaos but still functions, right-brained.

In the world of science (fictionalized), Crick and Watson

are shown in the film *Life Story* to be more right-brained and intuitive than poor, methodical, unemotional Rosalind Franklin who had the discovery of DNA 'stolen' from her.

Watson, in particular, has been made out as something of a hothead.

The big flaw in left-brain/right-brain theory is that it supposes you are born with a leaning towards one side or the other. In other words, what steers you towards the sciences or the arts is nature rather than a good teacher.

This is not true.

Or it is only partially true. While some people are clearly more imaginative than others, there is a consensus view that we are all born brimming with creativity. It just gets hammered out of us.

Sir Ken Robinson argues eloquently that our education system continues to provide our children with an education that was perfect for the 1880s. In the twenty-first century it is woefully out of kilter with our very modern problems and our very modern needs.

His TED talk 'Do schools kill creativity?'[12] has been watched over ten million times.

In Victorian times, primary schools were established to give a basic education to all children mainly so the brighter ones could be spotted and shunted further down the line.

They were taught to understand the technology of the day. They knew how to make the machines work which powered the Imperial economy.

If they were lower-middle class, then there was a prosperous middle class that provided the doctors and the accountants to keep the show on the road.

The public schools churned out the elite who went off around the world to manage it.

Today, our schools are ramming our children's left brains full of stuff and ignoring the other hemisphere.

Summer is ruined by annual exams the state demands you sit from the age of four through to twenty-one or twenty-two, when you take finals.

The exercise of imagination is actively discouraged.

This is Tim's story.

He studied English at Cambridge, where he shrugged off the dead hand of F. R. Leavis and forensic literary criticism.

For his thesis, he chose to write about *The Life and Opinions of Tristram Shandy, Gentleman*, written between 1759 and 1766 by Laurence Sterne.

It is an extraordinary book, which defies pigeon-holing. It's a bit of a ramble, very funny in some places, deliberately provocative in others. (It was the subject of the 2005 film *Cock and Bull Story*, with Steve Coogan and Rob Brydon.)

Now, Sterne is an anagram of Ernest. That gave Tim an idea. He titled his thesis 'The Importance of Being Sterne', referring, of course, to Oscar Wilde's great play *The Importance of Being Earnest*. Then he wrote 20,000 words about Lawrence Sterne in rhyming couplets, as if he was Oscar Wilde in Reading gaol.

Brilliant. Hilarious.

Fail.

He was told, you can't fool around with literature.

Why not?

Who says you can't?

Left-brained people, that's who.

The trouble is, left-brained thinking is dominant. It is *reasonable*. It follows, then, that if you manage to resist the educators and you do want to do things differently, you are unreasonable.

Certainly. Many creative people do feel at odds with the world.

If you like having ideas, if you like experimentation, then you are already a round peg in a square hole. You will already have discovered for yourself that there are plenty of people who are anti-creative.

In her 2011 TV show *Queen of Frocks*, Mary Portas told House of Fraser managers they were ignoring a massively important target group: women in their forties.

They wanted to look stylish and colourful. They wanted pizzazz. And they resented being made to look and feel frumpy.

Portas designed a range of clothes that went flying off the rails of House of Frasers everywhere. It turned out she was right. Middle-aged women did not want to dress for invisibility.

They much preferred pepper to vanilla.

In a little cutaway scene, one of the store's sales staff was asked how she felt about the success of the new lines. She hated it and couldn't wait for the store to go back to being normal, quiet, slow.

It came as no surprise when, in 2014, it was bought out by the Chinese company Sanpower.

It's a shock to find the word 'anti-creative' exists. In the dictionary, it's defined as 'opposed to originality of thought or the display of imagination'.

There's a lot of it out there.

The father who tells his son he won't pay the fees if the boy insists on going to art school.

The teacher who counsels caution.

The businessman who says, well, it always worked in the past.

The assistant at House of Fraser who says, this is how we do things here.

These are enemies of creativity.

But, here's the rub. They are anti-creative for the very best of reasons.

Son, I don't want you throwing your life away on a pipe dream.

My friend, if you buck the system here, the system will spit you out. And now you have a wife and a family . . .

All too often the people around you will find more reasons for not doing something than they will for doing it.

Why rock the boat?

Why fix it when it ain't bust?

The answer to these very human questions is simple.

There are two ways in which change happens. Either you invite it in or it engulfs you. Adapt or die.

Now, if you're all for change and you are excited by all things new, then you belong to a minority.

A well-known neuroscientist has said, off the record, that only one in five people is wired to be able to have an idea. In other words, four out of five people can replicate an idea but they simply can't come up with a new one.

I have mentioned this to neurologists and behavioural psychologists and they howl with rage. Creative people, on the other hand, find it comforting, as they have spent their entire lives being misunderstood and rebuffed. When you design something completely new, it's very hard for other people to understand exactly what you've done.

The people who have money mostly only want to buy what they are familiar with.

Arguably, much innovation happens despite the organization rather than because of it.

Are you a wild duck?

Just a little over twenty years ago, the charismatic businessman Lou Gerstner took over as CEO of IBM. At the time, the company was struggling and the *Wall Street Journal*, among others, told him in print he needed to break the company up and sell it to give the shareholders back some value. He chose not to follow this advice and decided instead to back his own people to transform the organization.

He recognized that there was an anti-creative culture at the very heart of IBM born from the old adage that 'no one ever got fired for buying IBM'. It had led to a dangerous complacency within the company.

The thing about change is that you may not be changing but everyone else around you is. Computing was moving to the laptop. And IBM wasn't.

Gerstner set about changing the culture knowing that if he could achieve that, his brightest people would change the products. He talked about 'wild ducks'.

He asked the rhetorical question, 'What do you do when you see a wild duck?'

Exactly. You shoot it.

Every day, he said, people walk into their offices in IBM and they say things like, 'You know, I've been thinking . . .' and everybody groans. So Gerstner addressed the entire workforce and asked them all to start thinking. If anyone had a good idea, he told them, 'take it to your manager. If he won't listen to you, take it to your manager's manager. And if he won't listen, then bring it to me.'

Soon there were stories of blue-collar guys being flown to New York on the company jet to share their ideas with the CEO.

In 1994 IBM launched Simon, the first smartphone.

It bombed after six months. Perhaps it was ahead of its time. It needed recharging after an hour of heavy use and it weighed a solid pound.

What it demonstrated, though, was that IBM wasn't just in the business of mainframes. Its wild ducks were beginning to fly.

Or, as Gerstner said in his first weeks as CEO of the company, 'the elephant must learn to dance'. And dance it still does.[13]

When I run training programmes, I sometimes get people to walk around the room and quack in honour of Gerstner. Quacking looks and sounds ridiculous, but if you have the front to look and sound ridiculous and actually enjoy it, then you're the person who might transform your company.

One young executive I got to quack worked for a big water company. He had been working for months on a plan to create an education centre on one of the company's reservoirs. He had a series of justifications for doing this. And he had all the costs.

He was given a slot at the next board meeting to pitch the idea. He lasted less than a minute.

'I'm here today to ask for £1.3 million to create an education centre on one of our major reservoirs and I'll share with you why I believe we should be doing this, what the benefits are, as well as the costs.'

The chairman, a big, bald individual, looked up briefly from the board papers.

'No.'

The young executive picked up his papers.

And made a little, quiet quack.

The chairman's head jerked up.

'What?'

'I think that's something to do with me,' interjected the marketing director. 'We recently had a training course where we talked about wild ducks. When any of us had an idea shot down, we were told to quack.'

'Are you telling me I just shot down an idea?'

'Well . . .'

The chairman invited the young exec to begin his presentation again. This time the board discussed it. As it happens, they didn't fund the project. Or at least, not right away. Two years later it did get the green light.

Quite possibly because someone quacked.

2:

HOW TO BE CREATIVE AS AN INDIVIDUAL

You have to want to be creative

A condition of creativity is that you (probably) have a wider range of interests than most of the people you know.

You are more interested in meanings and interpretations than in facts and figures.

You are curious.

And you are brave in as much as you know you are regarded as a bit eccentric or even a bit batty.

Psychologically, you are precisely the sort of person who interested Abraham Maslow.

In 1943, he stated that 'The story of the human race is the story of men and women selling themselves short.'

Rephrased, if you can explore your innate creativity and make more of it, there is every chance you will be more fulfilled in your life – and happy.

Maslow, of course, is famous for his 'hierarchy of needs' pyramid (*see overleaf*).[14]

Starting at the base of the pyramid, if our most basic physiological needs aren't met, then none of the mental states above are relevant.

Food, drink, sleep and sex. Those are the basics.

If people are starving, for instance, they become oblivious to danger as they are driven only by the need to find food. Moving up the pyramid, safety is about feeling secure

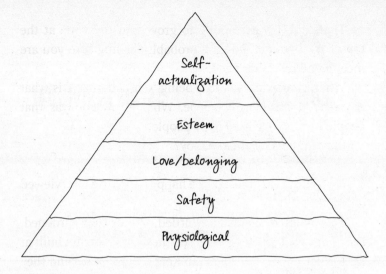

in your work and in your relationships. It's a state you feel most keenly in its absence. When you lose all your money, when you lose your home, when you lose your family, then you are going to be riven with insecurity.

Belongingness is interacting with others, being part of a community. Again, the absence of love/belonging is loneliness and depression.

Esteem is more than love; it is being valued for who we are and what we are. In this state, confidence soars and there is nothing you can't do.

You know the phrase, if you want something done, ask a busy person to do it for you? That person will be living in the Esteem zone.

Now, Maslow called these four levels 'deficiency needs'. They are necessities if we are to live in anything approaching physical and psychological comfort. All of these lesser needs have to be fulfilled before you can even approach the Self-actualization zone at the top.

That said, by attempting to grow into the zone at the top of the pyramid, you are probably making sure you are meeting all the other needs.

What Maslow says is that being 'self-actualized' is what any person can be. *Should* be. What he meant was that people in this zone are happy people.

But what makes them happy?

What's the secret sauce?

It turns out that most of the happy people he interviewed *did* stuff.

They painted, sketched, whittled, wrote. They gardened, they built walls (you can still see the wall Churchill built at his former house, Chartwell, in Kent), they sowed and they reaped.

Maslow himself came from a poor background.

He had an absentee father and a mother who seems to have been both cruel and deranged. Nevertheless, despite the unpromising start, he had, by his own admission, a successful and happy life.

Today, academics we have never heard of and who will never trouble the pages of a popular newspaper, enjoy Maslow-bashing.

'Where's the empirical evidence?' they ask.

What Maslow did – and why his hierarchy has established such a firm hold on the imagination – was to describe a sense of possibility.

So, the key questions to ask yourself are:

— What makes you happy?

— What are you doing when you feel most contented?

— What are your possibilities?

Finding answers to these may help you improve your life immeasurably. They are big questions, and not easy to answer off the top of your head. So, maybe a good way to start the process of opening up your own potential is to ask, who are your heroes?

Creative heroes

Art Fry is a creative hero and here's why.

He was at 3M, part of a team trying to create a glue so powerful it could stick together the steel plates of an ocean-going ship. The glue they came up with was, in one sense, a failure. It wouldn't stick a handle to a teacup.

But Art had a hunch.

Intuition is vital in creativity. It comes from years of acquiring knowledge and skills.

Art's intuition told him there was something in this unsticky glue. He just wasn't sure what. In church one Sunday, when his mind was wandering, he thought how he would like to be able to pre-programme his hymnbook.

Wouldn't it be good if he could put pieces of paper in the pages of the book so he could turn immediately to the next hymn?

Leaving this thought parked somewhere in his brain, he applied for engineering help. He wanted to prototype his idea and see what people did with almost-sticky pieces of paper.

He put up with his colleagues teasing him.

They couldn't understand what he saw in a glue that didn't work.

Art didn't know what he saw either.

But he was stubborn. And he was patient.

He had to wait two years to get his turn with the engineers.

When he did get to make his prototypes, he didn't sleep for three days.

So he was tenacious as well.

He still wasn't sure what he'd got so he left the sticky notes around the office and watched what happened.

So he learned and he adapted.

Then he went to his bosses and explained what he had done and why he thought there would be a market for his stickies.

'But the machinery set-up is complicated and expensive,' said the nay-sayers.

'Terrific,' replied Art. 'It means no one will want to copy us.'

So he was optimistic as well.

The bosses were iffy but eventually they gave the green light to Post-it Notes, now a trademarked name.

Art never moaned and groaned that he hadn't been paid enough for his idea.

His satisfaction was in his work.

He wore a tie pretty much every day of his working life.

In a crowd, he could have been mistaken for a librarian.

But look at those adjectives again.

Stubborn, persistent, patient, open, optimistic, driven not by a desire to extract value but to create value.

Here's another creative hero, as described by Malcolm Gladwell in 'The Creation Myth'.[15]

Gary Starkweather.

Now Starkweather, Gladwell suggests, may have been something of a handful for his managers.

Not because he was someone who had ideas. Rather because he was someone who had too many ideas.

His 'thing' was lasers.

He worked for Xerox in Webster, New York, which was where he first had the idea of running a document straight from a computer into a printer by laser.

What he wanted to do was take the information that made up a digital image and transmit it directly to a copier.

When he discussed the idea with his boss, it did not get a thumbs-up.

Starkweather, undeterred, kept at it.

He had to work in secret because he was told his whole team would be laid off if the laser idea wasn't dumped there and then.

Then Starkweather got to hear about Xerox PARC.

He asked to transfer from the East Coast to the West Coast.

He had to fight to get his bosses to agree to it.

But once he arrived in Palo Alto he picked up on his laser-printing idea until his new bosses agreed to an open competition between three teams.

Starkweather knew he would win.

And he did.

When he prototyped a laser printer using an existing Xerox 7000, again the bosses said no.

When he saw how lasers could print onto glass, he imagined Xerox could move into the semi-conductor business making 'masks'.

His bosses said no.

Looking back on his experiences, though, Starkweather himself remembers it as a time of excitement and growth rather than of frustration and dismay.

After nearly twenty-five years with Xerox he went to work at Apple, where he thought his ideas would be given free rein.

They weren't.

But the picture Gladwell gives of Starkwell in retirement is of someone still fizzing with energy and curiosity. A happy man.

The characteristics of the self-actualized person

Starkwell was convinced he was right.

He worked in secret.

He disobeyed his lords and masters.

He fought to get a transfer.

He competed openly with other teams.

He was utterly confident he would win.

He turned his big idea into something so big no one could see the size of it.

He did not sit on his laurels.

He moved on almost immediately to new opportunities to have ideas.

So, if you think there are advantages in life for creative people, how do you set out becoming one of them, when your school, university and even your own family have worked hard to make you a conformist?

Well, maybe by identifying a creative hero of your own and doing as they do or did.

In Chapter 4 (Write something, anything, pages 118–24) you can read about how copying ideas is a perfectly valid way to grow a business. It is an equally valid way to map out a career for yourself.

Who could be your creative hero?

What characteristics does that person have?

How might you develop some of those characteristics yourself?

What might you find yourself doing that would be so absorbing you would work late, work secretly, work determinedly?

My own creative hero is an advertising creative director called John Webster.

He was a genius at creating characters for brands.[16]

Cresta Bear.

The Hofmeister bear.

An animated bear for Unison. He liked bears.

He liked penguins too. They appeared regularly in his TV commercials for John Smith's Bitter.

He invented the honey monster for Sugar Puffs.

He first brought Gary Lineker to Walker's Crisps.

He also made the *Guardian* 'Points of View' commercial, voted the best British ad of all time in one poll.

What I learned from him was the power of concentration.

I was walking past his office one day when he called out, 'Got a minute?'

Seven hours later I tottered out, exhausted. But in those seven hours we had created a campaign for Sony, featuring a robot with a moustache. It sold a lot of Sony products, shifted brand favourability and won a few awards.

As well as writing famous ad campaigns, John was a very good painter and a very good scriptwriter.

He wrote a story about an aardvark called Hamilton Mattress.

When the agency floated and he made quite a lot of

money, he spent a significant wodge of it getting Aardman Animations to turn his script into a film.

For my money, this version was funnier and more memorable than the Christmas Special that eventually ran on ITV.

John was also a wine maker. His very first wine won a silver medal at the Nice wine festival.

Now I will never be as skilful as John as a writer, art director or viticulturalist, but I have learned to *do* as much as possible.

To start a second curve, if you like.

You have to try to get ahead of the curve

Some people, like John Webster, 'start over' instinctively. They get excited by new possibilities.

A few years ago there was a letter written to *Campaign*, the UK's journal of the advertising scene.

In his mid-fifties, one of the print production team in a large multinational agency wrote bitterly that after twenty-five years with the company he had been 'let go'.

What sort of reward was that for loyalty and exemplary conduct? he asked.

A week later there was another letter, written by a print production manager of a similar age in a similar agency.

He wrote that he felt deeply sympathetic to the other man but that five or six years earlier he had realized the industry was changing.

He wasn't sure how or why, but he had read somewhere that Adobe were creating software that was going to transform how print was created and distributed. So he got in touch.

Adobe were delighted to hear from him. Most agency people didn't want to listen to them. They simply couldn't see the writing on the wall.

They trained him. Made him a deal so he was able to get his agency to become early adopters of their technology and everyone did well from it.

They were all ahead of the curve.

But what exactly is this curve? Perhaps the best description of second-curve thinking and its value to both the individual and the organization is in the brilliant book *The Empty Raincoat*, written by business philosopher Charles Handy.[17]

Here he describes the Sigmoid Curve.

It is a wave shape.

It is a visual description of how empires rise and fall, of how love affairs bloom and fade, of careers that grow and crumble and of companies that come and go.

The curve starts with a period of experimentation and

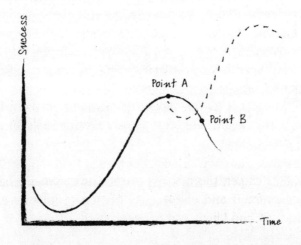

learning, then rises to a time of growth and prosperity, before it turns downwards and leads towards the end.

In any job, you start off not knowing what is expected of you.

Soon you get to grips with it.

You master it.

You become the go-to person whenever there is a question about it.

And that is the precise moment when you need to start a whole new curve of exploration and learning, which over time will lead to growth and prosperity when you must start again.

That is Point A on the Sigmoid Curve. It is the moment when everything is just falling into place.

It seems so unfair that it is precisely the moment you have to move on.

No basking in triumph.

No relaxing.

Because if you allow yourself to follow the trajectory, by the time you get to Point B it is too damn hard to haul yourself back to Point A. Or, more likely, those around you won't let you.

Handy talks about the French businessman who sold his family's successful textile business in order to open a chain of supermarkets.

Who knows if it was necessary? The businessman felt he *had* to start again in order to protect his children's future. So he did.

In my own career, there have been moments when I have reached Point B and change has occurred violently and unpleasantly and I have had to begin again.

I got fired.

I learned early on that it is easier to start again when you do not have an attachment to your past.

I have always been open to new ways of earning a living. However, I could have spared myself and my family a lot of anxiety if I had been the master of my own curve.

To do this, you have to learn to jump off at exactly the moment when you are most in control.

Some people have to be pushed.

Alan Parker was one of the finest copywriters of his generation. He worked at the most glamorous agency of the sixties and seventies, CDP.

He was summoned one day to the MD's office. Frank Lowe, now also a knight of the realm, stunned him by firing him.

But he immediately went on to say, 'But we have set you up with a production company. Go and direct commercials.'

Which he did.

Then he ran the second unit on a feature film for a friend, which set him off on the road to *Bugsy Malone* and the rest.

This is what you should do.

Draw the sideways S.

On that first upwards curve draw an ✗ to mark where you think you are right now in your job, enterprise or relationship.

Now get someone else to put an ✗ on the same curve marking where *they* think you are.

Almost always they'll put you further up than you put yourself.

You are closer to the jumping-off point than you think.

But that begs a question.

Jump off doing what?

Again, Handy offers some help here.

He writes about the 'doughnut' principle.

The centre of the doughnut, the core, is what you got hired to do. Your core competencies, if you like.

My brother Rob is a mountain guide.

He has to be able to climb mountains.

He can't wave goodbye to the climbers from base camp. He has to be able to lead a group, *any* group, of climbers up just about any sort of mountain.

The core, though, is not the whole doughnut.

In most jobs, where you get your satisfaction and where you are valued is in that outer space.

It's not *what* you do so much but *how* you do it.

Rob happens to be interesting company. He has climbed most of the world's major mountains. The reason he chose not to climb Everest is part of what makes him so engaging.

He is an ornithologist, a poet and a student of mountain literature.

Nowhere in the books does it say your mountain guide has to be a keen football fan but Rob discovered that being a Manchester United follower allowed him to start conversations with people.

Nowhere in the books does it say your guide should start quoting Edward Thomas to you as you gaze out at Wales spread below you.

Even though it makes the moment more memorable. Gives it a point.

Rob is also a good photographer. Taking photographs of the wilder and wetter parts of the world has given him pleasure.

One of his photographs, of a dry and stony valley in Afghanistan, was the *Observer*'s shot of the week.

It has also given him the means by which to interpret and explain his experiences.

He writes and gives lectures. I saw him in action at the Royal Geographic Society one evening. He described how the man he was climbing with slipped and fell when they were on a knife ridge. Without hesitation, Rob jumped the other way. There they were, on either end of the rope, dangling on opposite sides of the ridge. It took Rob several hours to calm the other climber and get him back onto the ridge and off it onto safer ground.

Nowhere in the job spec does it say mountain guides have to be storytellers.

Rob's second curve was to take his young family off to New Zealand, where he became manager of the Mount Cook National Park.

Returning to Wales, his third curve was to take a course to be a trainer.

Working out of the National Outdoor Centre at Plas y Brenin, he devised leadership programmes for company executives.

My favourite story of his time as a trainer of management skills was when he collected a group of senior executives from BP at Llandudno Junction railway station.

They had all come in wet-weather gear.

Cagoules, chunky sweaters, trainers.

When the minibus brought them to Plas y Brenin, Rob welcomed them by saying, 'You may have noticed some posters on the telegraph poles and on the walls in the villages coming up? They are for the play you are putting on in this hall on Saturday night.'

Map your own doughnut

Not all that long ago, I was in Australia doing a lecture tour.

In Sydney, after I'd been waving my arms around and shouting for forty-five minutes, a young man came up to me.

'You know what? I love living here in Australia. I've got a great job, my kids are healthy and outdoorsy in a way they never were back in London. And I've got your doughnut to thank for it.'

He'd attended one of my workshops and mapping his doughnut had led Jim to see that he wasn't making the most of himself.

Here's how you do it.

Draw a circle and a second circle within that.

Inside the core list those skills you *have* to have in your job. Without these you would fail.

Look at any jobs board online and the ads tell you what you *must* be able to do. But what gets you hired and gets you your rise is mostly down to what you do in the outer ring.

Here you should list all the things you do at work which are *not* in the job spec.

Maybe you put together the department five-a-side football team.

Perhaps you organize karaoke nights.

What are the additional skills you bring to the job, the attributes that determine *how* you do the job?

Back in the day, I hired an architect to be a copywriter.

It was a bit of a risk but Mark C. had impressed me with his can-do attitude. From the start he did not disappoint.

I had asked him to work on a well-known laundry brand. They were looking for a new campaign.

Mark wrote some scripts, which he showed me on a Friday morning.

I thought they showed promise.

I made some suggestions and fixed to see his improvements on Monday.

What he showed me weren't amended scripts.

He had rented a video camera and persuaded two of his mates to help him film a couple of demo ads.

That's what he showed me, two rough but visually remarkable commercials.

Where every laundry ad in the history of forever had shown nice white mums washing nice white school shirts, Mark went to Southall.

This London borough is home to a huge Asian community. Their washing lines are livid with colour. Saris and kameez in every hue.

Even though video cameras were now cheap to buy and easy to use, not a single so-called 'creative' in my creative department had had the gumption to use the one I had bought for them.

Here was Mark, beginning a second curve when his first curve still had a way to go before he got to Point A.

In the outer part of his doughnut were an interest in film; an interest in London.

As an architect, his interest in low-cost housing had taken him to the poorer parts of London, parts few of his peers had ever seen.

They just happened to be the more multicoloured parts.

Also in his outer ring would have been cheerful enthusiasm. And persuasiveness. How did he get a couple of friends to spend their weekend helping him in his job? And how did he persuade several Indian families to open up their homes and their gardens to him? Let alone their washing machines?

Mark is a second curver by nature.

What you put in your outer ring will be the interests and abilities that might inspire your second curve.

One merchant banker I knew reinvented himself as an importer of flowers. Another made enough money to be able to indulge in his real passion, teaching.

The Sunday papers have stories every week about marketers who opened up cupcake shops, or executives who walked away from success to risk failure with a start-up.

One ad executive I know started a mail-order ballet shoe business, and it's doing very nicely, thank you.

James Heneage left advertising, where he would almost certainly have risen to the top, to open a bookshop. Which grew into Ottakar's, at one time a chain of 141 shops.

Have a pause. Think for a moment if there is someone you know who started a second curve? Could you do the same?

Understanding your outer ring isn't just about how you might be able to reinvent yourself, it is also about protecting yourself.

No one has a job for life any longer.

In fact, few people have single careers.

We are all having to learn how to be plural. To have multiple careers.

When companies 'restructure' or when there's a 're-org', jobs go.

In looking for the people to 'let go', whether they mean to or not, managers and bosses judge their people by what they have in the outer ring.

Everyone satisfies the core skills.

So how do you choose to keep one person and lose another?

By *how* they do the job.

By the elements within the outer doughnut.

So, when you start jotting down what those elements may be in your own case, write *everything*.

What are the things that rock your boat? Heavy metal? Mozart? Croquet? Cricket? Church architecture? English watercolours?

The things that look furthest from your core competencies may provide the starting point of a second curve.

Richard Venables was the managing director of Ogilvy & Mather. When he took early retirement, he became a maker of musical instruments. One of his violins is currently in the hands of the principal violinist with the Royal Philharmonic.

I've created a doughnut for myself. To be honest, I think it looks more like a fried egg and the analogy of the yolk and the albumen together making a wholesome meal makes more sense than a ring of dough with a hole in the middle. But Charles Handy calls it a doughnut and who am I to argue with the great man?

At the centre are all the things I *have* to do to keep from getting the sack. In the outer ring, though, are all the things that I *do* do, and while they seem unconnected to the day job, in fact they are fundamental to it.

What's more, they also provide pointers to my future, either within the company or outside it, should I choose to go back to working for myself again.

Just looking at the second ring gives me ideas about setting up a YouTube channel and becoming a content creator.

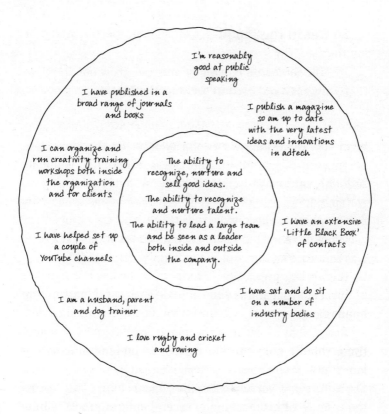

The ability to recognize, nurture and sell good ideas.
The ability to recognize and nurture talent.
The ability to lead a large team and be seen as a leader both inside and outside the company.

I'm reasonably good at public speaking

I have published in a broad range of journals and books

I publish a magazine so am up to date with the very latest ideas and innovations in adtech

I can organize and run creativity training workshops both inside the organization and for clients

I have an extensive 'Little Black Book' of contacts

I have helped set up a couple of YouTube channels

I am a husband, parent and dog trainer

I have sat and do sit on a number of industry bodies

I love rugby and cricket and rowing

As far as I know, there is only one YouTuber over the age of sixty with any sort of following: the amazing Tricia Cusden. Perhaps there's room for another?

Perhaps I can start a vlog about dogs? Or a vlog about millennials from the boomer point of view and how very vexing they are to us?

You get the point, I hope.

When you write down all your attributes, not only do you begin to see what your value is to the organization, but you get to see what you might do to start a second curve.

Get in the mood

*'We don't stop playing because we grow old,
we grow old because we stop playing.'*
George Bernard Shaw

While I was working with John Webster on the Sony campaign (see pages 44–5), there was a moment when he suddenly sat forward and looked at me.

'Isn't it amazing?' he ventured. 'Someone is actually paying us to do this.'

What he managed to do when he was working on a brief was to create an atmosphere of jokey playfulness.

Banter was important.

It meant that status was set aside and I could talk to him as an equal.

Being able to get into the mood for creativity is something that Donald MacKinnon began investigating in the late 1960s. If you haven't got time to read MacKinnon's book *The Nature and Nurture of Creative Talent*, John Cleese distils the essence of his teaching in several entertaining YouTube videos.[18]

MacKinnon wrote that the human brain works in two very distinct ways: open and closed. When the mind is open to new ideas, it is relaxed, playful, questing. The moment it latches on to an idea it reverses and becomes closed. It uses all the formidable powers of intellect to validate what it has just thought.

Open is a childlike state in which you explore ideas for no immediate practical purpose but for the sake of enjoyment. Quite simply, it's fun to see where your thinking takes you.

Closed-mode thinking is purposeful, directed and about dealing with an immediate task. Trying to keep the mind in an open state for as long as possible so it can generate as many ideas as possible is what this book is all about.

Some creative people call this state daydreaming.

Art Fry, inventor of the Post-it Note (see pages 40–1), was allowing his mind to wander in church when he first came up with his idea about how to use a glue that wasn't very sticky.

It's what we all used to do in class as children. Until the duster came whizzing through the air to bring us back to reality.

'Wake up, boy!'

Einstein talked about creativity as 'the residue of time wasted'.

Therein lies the first problem.

One of the principles of creativity is that you have to be prepared for absolutely nothing to happen. The creative process does not always end up with a new product.

Some people simply can't do this.

They demand a result.

They can't bear to waste time.

Shut yourself away

One way of 'getting in the mood' seems to be through boredom.

In a 2012 essay in the *New Yorker*, Jonah Lehrer[19] describes a Harvard research study. A hundred and forty-five students were given a standard creativity test – one I often use myself – to come up with as many possible uses they could think of for a brick.

One group was deliberately given a break, in which nothing happened. They became bored. Their minds wandered.

When they were then asked to come up with new uses for a brick, they came up with 'forty one per cent more possibilities' than the other students.

So, find yourself what Cleese calls 'a fortress of solitude' – that place where the demands of the everyday can't get to you.

It could be the traditional man cave, the shed in the garden.

George Bernard Shaw's shed rotated so he could sit in the sun all day and write. Roald Dahl wrote his bestsellers in his shed, and Benjamin Britten wrote music in one too. Dylan Thomas wrote *Under Milk Wood* in a garage converted into a shed.

Some people seek solitude in the library.

One creative director I know walks miles around the London parks.

Do the things you did when you were young

This summer I lay in a field and looked up at clouds. I last did that when I was sixteen. And my mind began wandering. Which is when I first got the idea for a YouTube channel: oldies doing stuff youngsters think is their preserve.[20]

We've all laughed at how kids often get more pleasure out of the box their Christmas present comes in than in the present itself. Their imaginations turn the box into a fort, into a boat, into a robot. Observing this is one of the most rewarding aspects of parenthood. Your children encourage you to play games. Not only do you develop closer ties with each other, they are teaching you to unlearn corporate conservatism.

Get back into the habit of fooling around

I don't know about you, but when I was at school I was constantly being shouted at.

'Stop playing the fool, boy.'

The fool is disruptive. The fool calls things as he or she sees them. The fool has the nerve to tell the king he's wrong.

The fool uses humour to circumnavigate opposition.

He or she has the ability to come up with ideas that are strikingly absurd but, in their absurdity, work.

Odysseus was no fool. But what a bizarre idea to suggest that the Greeks should build a horse and leave it outside the gates of Troy.

'We'll hide some crack troops inside the horse and when the Trojans wheel the thing inside the city, we'll jump out and take the place from within.'

Which they did.

Stupid ideas can make you stupidly rich.

One of my favourites is the pet rock.

Gary Dahl invented it in 1975.[21]

Pet rocks needed no feeding or grooming. They would never throw up or be disobedient.

The thirty-two-page booklet he wrote that went in every box was hilarious.

He sold one and a half million pet rocks at $4 each.

The Snuggie is a more recent retail phenomenon. Twenty million of these blanket-cum-romper suits have sold at around $20 a throw, allowing inventor Scott Boilen to laugh all the way to the bank.

Humorous advertising was fundamental to its success.

The Snuggie is not the sort of idea you have if you set out in all seriousness to achieve.

It is the sort of idea you can only have if you enjoy fooling around.

So, here's how to fool around:

- Become deliberately contrarian. See what happens when you zig when everyone else is zagging.

    You will really get up other people's noses. But that's the whole point. As the fool you will start arguments which flush out what people really believe, including you.

    You're not being bloody-minded. You are flexing your brain. You are breaking habits.

- Do a Duke. This is Duke Ellington, musician and composer. He once said, 'I began by tinkering with some old tunes I knew. Then, just to try something different, I set to putting some music to the rhythm that I used in jerking ice-cream sodas at the Poodle Dog. I fooled around with the tune more and more until at last, lo and behold, I had completed my first piece of finished music.'[22]

    That's pretty good advice.

    Look at the product or service you offer. Then think about all the other products out there like yours. Start riffing off them, what they do and how they do it, and see how that changes how you think of your own offering.

- Be prepared to be completely wrong. And to make mistakes. But also know that when you do cock up you need to clean up quickly and move on.

- Accept that there is no single answer to the problem you are dealing with. There may be dozens of solutions. How to get them to reveal themselves is the challenge.

- Embrace the paradoxical world we live in. You have to understand all the old ideas in order to have a new one. Actively look for paradox and see what ideas don't come bubbling up as a result.

  Saint Francis said, 'In giving we receive.' So, what can you give away? And what might the consequences of the act of giving be?

  Being a creative person is paradoxical in itself. To be a revolutionary you need to be fully aware of all the institutions of government. In 1789, it was the lawyers who brought down the French monarchy, not the peasantry.

- Look out for the ridiculous. Every day you will come across something utterly bonkers. Photograph it and share it.

  For instance, I once saw a poster with this headline: 'Are you illiterate?'

  Driving in France, we came to a T-junction. The sign to the left was marked 'Espagne'. The sign to the right was marked 'Espagne'.

- Keep your eyes open. Here's a little exercise to try.

  Take your mobile phone. Walk outside. In a radius of just 300 yards, see how many faces you can find – in the cracks in the wall, in the oil stains on the car park. It's called pareidolia.

When you start looking, it doesn't take long before you're smiling.

The artist Graham Fink had an exhibition of pareidolic photographs which was a joy.[23]

- Laugh. Laugh at your own foibles; laugh when other people notice your foibles. Laugh when things go wrong because the people with you will start to laugh too. And you become determined as a group to put it right.

  Your stress levels come down. Your energy levels go up.

You have to give it time

This book is full of suggestions of things to do that might help you have an idea or two.

The challenge is how do you devote hours, days and even weeks to an activity that may not yield a result? And the one thing we all have in common these days is a scarcity of time.

I asked a group of executives I was consulting with to keep a work diary for two weeks. There was nothing scientific about it. Nevertheless, the data I collected was an eye-opener.

It turned out that, on average, they all spent about 45 per cent of their working week on admin. Seventy per cent of that was on reporting up to the boss.

By and large, most bosses will add to your workload

rather than lighten it. What it meant was that these executives each had just eighteen hours a week to do the job.

So, when I ask you to fool around, I know how difficult it will be.

However, Warren Buffet claims to spend 80 per cent of his time reading and thinking. It's how he has built one of the largest companies in the USA.

Tim Armstrong at AOL is said to insist his top executives spend half a day a week just thinking.

Bill Gates takes a week off twice a year to go into retreat, to think.

Felix Dennis claimed that he hired a cleaner when he was just seventeen. Even that young, he had figured out that time spent doing chores was time taken out of his mission to be massively rich.

Hiring people to do what he didn't want to do helped give him the time to do what he did best. That was creating magazines, starting with *Kung Fu Monthly*, taking in *PC World* and extending to *Maxim*.

10,000 hours of practice

In *Outliers*, Malcolm Gladwell punts the notion that success comes to those who manage to put in 10,000 hours of practice first.

He describes how Bill Gates spent 10,000 hours writing code before he launched Microsoft.

In a YouTube video, *Bill Gates on Expertise*, Gates agrees that luck and timing are important elements of success.[24] He was born at exactly the right time to take advantage of new discoveries about microprocessors. But he put the hours in to learn everything there was to know about this aspect of computing.

Gladwell describes a study of violinists conducted in Germany.

The researchers discovered that the elite performers had put in around 10,000 hours of practice by the time they were twenty. The also-rans averaged 4,000 hours.

The violinists who rose to the top were not endowed with a natural gift above and beyond the others. They got to the top through hard work.

He notes also that when the Beatles went to Hamburg, they played in tiny venues pretty much non-stop.

By 1964 they had already played 1,200 gigs, often performing for as long as eight hours a night, seven days a week.

It seems they practised more than any band in history.

Which is what allowed them to make history.

Johnny Wilkinson became famous for his obsession with goal kicking. As a child, he had rugby posts in his garden so he could practise. As a professional player he was usually the last off the training pitch.

Ten thousand hours of smacking a ball over a bar allowed him to score 1,179 points for England in the Six Nations tournament. No one has scored more.

Jono H. is a talented portrait painter. One day, a young woman stood behind him as he sketched her friend. 'That's amazing,' she cooed. 'I don't know how you do it.'

'Oh, it's easy,' he told her. 'You do it once, then you do it another thousand times and it all begins to come together.'

A lot of people think being able to draw is a gift. Jono knew that it is an interest followed by perseverance.

Remember the Gary Player story (also attributed to Jack Nicklaus, Arnold Palmer, Ben Hogan, et al): the harder I practise the luckier I get.

The questions to ask yourself are:

— Is there anything I do and which I like doing so much I have done it 10,000 times?

— Is there anything I want to do so much I can imagine doing it 10,000 times?

If you have a 'yes' to either of those, then you have arrived at a fork in the road.

It is no surprise, then, that creative people are often described as brave.

Creativity can be learned. However, you do have to *want* to explore your potential. You have to be a *bit* curious about the world. You do *need* to be open to new experiences and new ideas.

Open yourself up to new experiences

Is creativity utterly arbitrary?

Is it luck?

The way you were wired when you were born?

Or is it all about chance?

Mihály Csíkszentmihályi describes a famous painter, who believed his stellar career was all thanks to a lucky break.

He met someone at a party.

They got on well.

They became friends.

The man he met went on to become an art dealer.

As a dealer, he did what he could to promote his pal.

A rich investor bought one of his paintings. Which led a museum to want one too. Which led to the retrospective.

Which led to the headlines. And to the ever-increased value of his canvasses.

Total accident.

Except, of course, it wasn't.

Creative people have a knack for putting themselves in the way of possibilities. Quite often they are able to look the other way down the telescope. They are 'counterfactual'.

For instance, where most of us would say after a car accident, 'That was awful, I had a prang,' the creative person says, 'Wow! I was lucky not to get injured in that crash.'

Someone I know thinks the luckiest day of his life was the day he ran into another car in London.

It so happened the other driver was a beautiful girl.

'I would never have had the bottle to approach her at a party or in a bar but standing there waiting for the police to arrive it seemed the most natural thing in the world to ask her out for a date.'

They were married a year later.

Can you actually learn to notice things? Can you learn how to make new and surprising connections?

Can you become more curious?

I think you can but you have to set out wilfully to break the patterns of your day-to-day life.

For example, try something as simple as going a different way to work.

You will find it harder to do than you imagine.

My route to work involves a twenty-mile drive, a train into the city, the Tube for two stops and then a five-minute walk.

Every single part of it can be done differently.

I can drive to a station closer to home, which would

give me a longer train journey but more time to read and reflect.

When I get into London, I can use a Boris bike to get to the office. Or walk. It takes about half an hour but if the sun is up, crossing Russell Square is pleasant.

Every morning I have a choice.

I can give myself up to routine and travel in a state of anaesthetized indifference. Or I can force myself to think about where I am going and how I might get there.

Remember this: there are more reasons for *not* doing something than there are for doing it.

Most people really don't like doing it different.

You included.

Me included.

Breaking the pattern means you become more aware of yourself and the environment around you.

Inevitably, it means you start noticing things.

Maybe you see things you have never seen before.

Walking from St Pancras to Soho, I came across Woburn Walk with its lovely bow-fronted houses.[25] This little street looks as it must have done a hundred and fifty years ago. Surrounded by ghastly post-modern splat architecture, it's a little oasis of elegance.

Online I learned it had been built in 1822 as London's first purpose-built pedestrian street.

It also happens to be where W. B. Yeats lost his virginity.

Is this useful to know?

Not yet. But maybe one day.

Doing it different opened up a small but interesting line of enquiry that took in architecture, literature and historical drama. I started looking out for Woburn Walk on TV, whenever there was a series set in Victorian London. And, gosh, it gets used a lot. The people who live there must make a fortune in location fees.

And that prompted me to get in touch with a location scout.

Maybe the director of a TV drama will like the look of our barn and want to use it. Which could help pay for the landscaping we want to do.

Read a magazine you've never read before

Sometimes, I send people out of my workshops at lunchtime to buy a magazine or a newspaper they have never read before. Then I get them to read it and report to the group what they have learned.

Firstly, it is fascinating to see how many people choose a magazine or paper they *might* read if they hadn't already made their brand choices.

A reader of *The Times* might try the *Guardian*.

A reader of *Cosmo* might read *Red*.

They can't break their habits.

Some, though, come back with round eyes.

They can't believe how many magazines there are in the university bookshop up the road. Even WHSmith has hundreds of titles on show.

When you open up any one of them, you open up a new world.

And it can be amazing.

One of my workshoppers picked up *The Caterer*.

In it he found a story tucked away about a French chef. It mentioned that he had been awarded two Michelin stars for the restaurant he ran somewhere in the Midi. But he had packed up and he had come to Britain because he believed his food would be better appreciated on this side of the Channel.

Of all the places he could have chosen to open up, he had chosen Scunthorpe.

'Scunthorpe,' he told *The Caterer*, 'will be the gastronomic centre of Europe.'

Was he prescient? Or deluded?

Either way, the bathos of the story makes it intriguing, the subject for a sitcom, perhaps, or a novel about thwarted ambition.

Try it.

Widen your understanding of how other people live their lives.

Buy the magazine *Sheep!*.

Yes, it really exists.

How about *Cranes Today*?

Sadly, the *Croquet Gazette* has folded. But think of a sport, any sport, and there will be a magazine for it.

Morticians Monthly is published in America but a friend spotted a copy on a news stand in New York and brought it back for me.

Full-page ads for coffins. Articles about embalming technologies.

And, because I am sick, my favourite page: the obituaries.

'We say goodbye to fellow morticians . . .'

Extend the principle to listen to a radio station you've never listened to before.

Find a TV channel and watch it.

One friend emailed me in excitement when he discovered Luxe TV. This is video of hotel lobbies, streamed twenty-four hours a day.

There used to be a channel that played a log fire and nothing else – for people who wanted the log-fire effect in their living rooms without actually having a log fire.

Choose a film at random.

Go to a museum or gallery.

If you've never eaten Turkish, Lebanese, Moroccan, Senegalese food, find a Turkish, Lebanese, Moroccan or Senegalese restaurant.

Try rollmop herring.

Actually, on second thoughts, don't.

But you get the picture.

You can institutionalize this.

In *Sticky Wisdom*, Fergal Quinn is reported as allocating a different food-related magazine from around the world to every person who works for his Superquinn chain of supermarkets.[26]

They have to read it and ping him details of anything they find interesting or relevant to the business.

Try something new for breakfast

On the subject of different cuisines, when I ran creativity workshops, attendees would turn up at our location expecting breakfast.

We had made sure it was advertised on the agenda we sent out days before.

> *8.30 a.m. Breakfast*
> *9.00 a.m. Start*

Everyone imagined breakfast would be croissants and muffins.

Maybe even some scrambled eggs, a bit of bacon and a banger.

We served up red wine and cheese.

A mild curry on one occasion.

Maybe steak and ale seemed peculiar to those who were offered it first thing but only because habit has petrified their understanding of what a good breakfast is. In Regency times, a gentleman usually began his day with steak and ale.

We dished up hot chocolate and waffles one morning.

Actually, most of the attendees enjoyed it after the initial, automatic rejection.

In the seventeenth century, the well-to-do almost always had chocolate first thing. It took time for coffee and tea to catch on.

And, as for waffles, King Edward VII had crêpes for breakfast throughout most of his life.

Funnily enough, strawberries and cream at 8 a.m. was a harder ask.

Try it in your workplace.

For no other reason than to see what happens.

It's a great way to start a conversation, by the way.

What is the weirdest thing you have ever eaten?

Fried crocodile egg for me. And once was enough.

In *Cannery Row*, John Steinbeck's cheerful tale of poor white trash in 1940s California, Doc has always wondered what a beer milkshake would taste like.

Every time he has a beer, which is often, he wonders if

mixing it with milk would make it curdle? Would it need sugar?

Doc knows that if he ordered a beer milkshake in a town where he wasn't known, they would call the police.

The only way he can satisfy his curiosity is to pretend he has been prescribed it for medical reasons.

As it turns out, beer milkshake doesn't taste great. But it doesn't taste awful either. Just like flat beer with milk.

The moral of this little story is, when you break a pattern, expect everyone else to be shocked and even hostile to both the idea and to you.

Doing it different requires effort.

You're bucking the trend.

You're a square peg in a round hole.

You're a paid-up member of the awkward squad.

And that, of course, is part of the secret of creativity – learning to *enjoy* being different.

Meet a stranger on a train

At the earliest age, you are told never to talk to strangers, yet 'Hello' can be a magic word. If you start a conversation with a stranger, you're breaking out of your bubble.

And, again, you could be putting yourself in the way of an experience.

My friend Tim was an out-of-work actor.

He had done a few commercials, had played a padre in a WWII TV drama but had never got the phone call from Hollywood or from the Royal Shakespeare Company.

But he was (is) also a writer.

On a ferry to France he fell into conversation with a man, who turned out to be a playwright.

The plays he wrote were of a very particular nature. They were used for training workshops. A particular problem would be set up by the drama. Then the audience would break out into groups to discuss and plan how the problem could be solved. The actors then improvised the final act and found a resolution.

Today, Tim is the co-owner of an extremely successful training-through-theatre company. He writes plays to help workers on oil rigs understand how dangerous situations arise and how to deal with them.

Architects know how important a serendipitous meeting can be. Apple HQ is said to be designed so people with different skillsets will bump into each other.

Many new tech companies have large coffee stations where people can meet and talk while they rustle up a cappuccino.

Improbable things don't just happen occasionally, they happen all the time.

The psychologist Carl Jung was fascinated by this and called it 'synchronicity'.[27]

Some people seem to have meaningful coincidences more frequently than others, because they put themselves out there.

Go a different way.

Eat a different meal.

Read a different paper.

Start a conversation with a stranger.

What you may be doing is creating the conditions in which a remarkable change of fortune can happen.

3:

HOW TO BE A CREATIVE MANAGER

This is a time of opportunity

Abraham Maslow put creativity into two categories.

First-class creativity was when you had an invention or a discovery on your hands that changed everything. Often invention was down to one person with a huge leap of the imagination.

Second-class creativity was what happened in laboratories and engineering departments. Hundreds, even thousands, of drones were tasked with designing efficiencies to the inventions.

Top tier ideas are few and far between, though there is evidence they may be occurring more rapidly now than at any other time in history, partly because technology has empowered more people to have new ideas and partly because there are more problems to be solved.

In 1997, *Focus* magazine polled its readers, mostly boffins of one sort or another. They were asked to nominate what they thought the most important ideas in history have been.

The end list was:

1. Sanitation
2. The computer
3. The printing press

4. Fire

5. The wheel

6. Antibiotics

7. The Internet

8. The transistor

9. The laser

10. Contraception

Elsewhere in the list was plastic at number 12, flight at number 14, the electric light at 23, the car at 15, the map at 28, money at 29, the telephone at 34 and photography at 38.[28]

Every one of those was a big idea. A really big idea. Each begat an entire industry unto itself. And each industry is worth billions.

Other, lesser inventions of the last seventy years include:

— The TV remote in 1955 (which my wife reckons to be the most useful invention of them all).

— The microwave oven (1955).

— The pill (1957). Wow, just think how that has changed relationships, changed culture, changed societies.

— The first satellite, Telstar (1962).

— Drones, suddenly mass market now but first invented in 1964.

— The smoke alarm (1965).

— The personal computer. The Commodore Pet came out in 1977.

— GPS (1978).

— DNA fingerprinting (1984).

And so on.

The chances are, no one reading this has come up with, or is about to invent, anything of this scale.

Rather most business today is driven by innovation.

Bringing improved performance and effectiveness to existing ideas.

The two most valuable companies in the world right now, Apple and Google, didn't actually invent anything.

Okay, they will protest that they have a million and one patents between them to prove they are inventing day in, day out.

Still, I'd say they are innovators.

There were already laptops before the MacBook. There was the Walkman before the iPod. There were mobile phones before the iPhone.

Yellow Pages helped people find information. Do you remember Alta Vista? Ask Jeeves? They were pre-Google search engines before Larry Page and Sergey Brin found a way of doing it faster, deeper, better.

Innovation falls into two distinct camps.

There are start-ups, which come into being after the founders have had what they think is a good idea.

And there are existing companies who have to innovate in order to remain competitive in their markets.

In terms of start-ups, the *Daily Telegraph* reported that there were probably going to be over 600,000 new companies established in the UK in 2015, up from 581,000 in 2014.[29]

That's a new business born every minute.

Innovation, then, is the very lifeblood of British business.

And, for those with ideas, there has never been a better time to start up.

There is optimism and money.

And while Moore's Law may only apply to computing hardware, plenty of investors seem to think there is a continuing doubling of capability and a doubling of value across all new technologies.

(In 1965, Gordon Moore predicted that the processing power of computers of all sizes would double every two years thanks to the ability to double the number of transistors per square inch on their integrated circuit boards.)

Here are ten companies worth a billion dollars. What is astonishing is that none of these businesses existed five years ago.

Gusto – a cloud-based payroll system.

Udacity – an education portal that offers free classes.

Infinidat – a data storage company.

The Honest Company – non-toxic and eco-friendly baby products.

Human Longevity – a database for the human genome.

Instacart – grocery deliveries.

Avant – lends you money faster than any bank.

Oscar – revolutionizing health insurance.

Slack – a chat app.

Snapchat – valued at $20 billion in mid-2016, which must make twenty-five-year-old founder Evan Spiegel rub his eyes.[30]

Well, it makes me rub mine.

Innovation and the future of the planet

If we agree that creativity is the desire and ability to solve problems and that innovation is the means by which we can test the solutions in the real world, then we have some incredible opportunities both to make money and to make the world safer.

Starting with population growth.

The world will have a population of over nine billion by 2050.[31]

Already, just a handful of the problems associated with this growth are:

- Hunger
- The inability of agriculture to supply enough food for all those mouths
- The inability of the world to provide employment for all
- A widening of the gap between the haves and the have nots
- Increased illegal migration

Cascading out of the one problem of overpopulation come a host of other problems, such as:

- Food waste in first-world countries. In the UK, we throw away nearly 50 per cent of the food we buy.
- Global warming. More people consume more energy.
- Depletion of natural resources. What happens when oil and coal run out? And the Amazon has been turned to desert?

- Pollution of the seas, pollution of the air.

- Disease. Epidemics and pandemics.

- Mass extinction of species as they get crowded out of their habitats by people. Farewell the tiger, the rhino, the gorilla and the blue whale among others.

- Crime.

I could go on.

The big problem is that every little problem is connected another and each has consequences.

Together, those consequences pose some very real threats to us as people, as a society and as a species.

Ideas needed. Urgently.

How can you do what you did yesterday better today?

This book has already suggested a number of questions you might ask yourself. And here are two more, offered in the spirit of creativity.

In other words, they aren't questions with a yes or no answer. They are questions intended to broaden your thinking rather than narrow it down.

Answering the first question may help you define your attitude towards how you do things.

Answering the second may help you define what things you do.

Question one: ask yourself, how can I do what I did yesterday better today?

It doesn't matter how lowly or how elevated you are in the organization, if you can make a series of small changes, you will end up making a big difference.

As already mentioned, Sir Dave Brailsford turned Britain's uncompetitive cyclists into champions through 'marginal gains'.

Make a number of fractional improvements and you end up with a sizeable advantage.

At Ogilvy & Mather's London office, we got into the Gunn Report's top ten agencies in the world for creativity.[32]

I would like to take all the credit.

Actually, Mitch W. was as responsible as anyone for our creative success.

He was the traffic manager, responsible for the through-put of work. Historically, this was a job for someone who liked spreadsheets.

Mitch took it to a new level.

His big idea was to move his desk out of his office and into the corridor.

Every single person coming in and out of the department had to pass him by.

If the account people were trying to get a sneak peek at the work before the creative teams were ready, he would bare his teeth.

If the creatives were on their way out, he would make sure they knew they were expected back.

Brilliantly, he made sure all the work for a major pitch was ready a full twenty-four hours before the clients came in. That way everyone had time to familiarize themselves with it and prepare their parts of the presentation.

That is creativity.

Thinking, how can I do my job just a tiny bit better?

Then having an idea.

And doing it.

What business are we in?

The second question to ask is, what business are we in, *really*?

Theodore Levitt was a professor at Harvard University. In 1960 he published a paper in the *Harvard Business Review* called 'Marketing Myopia'.

He could see that many companies found it difficult to set themselves directions for innovation.

They spent time and money on ideas that were irrelevant to their future.

What Levitt had noticed was that in most industries, growth slowed down and even came to a grinding halt – not because the market had become mature, but because of a failure of its managers.

The premise of his book is that most companies simply don't know what business they are in.

Take the White Star Line.

In 1913, it was one of the most prosperous companies in the world.

They had innovated furiously, moving from running a fleet of clippers to operating a fleet of steam-driven iron-clads.

Britannic, *Germanic*, *Teutonic* and *Majestic* all held the Blue Riband at some point, the label given to the fastest crossing of the Atlantic.

Oceanic of 1899 was the first ship to be longer than Brunel's *Great Eastern*.

Cedric, Baltic and *Adriatic*, built between 1901 and 1904, carried over 2,000 passengers and over 17,000 tons of cargo.

Titanic was at the cutting edge of marine design before hubris did for her.

In 1934 White Star merged with Cunard.

By 1950 the name had disappeared.

What Levitt observed was that the directors of the company thought they were in the shipping business. Had they decided they were in the transportation business, they would have taken an interest in aviation.

And had they done that, today you could be flying in and out of Gatwick on a White Star jet.

It was the same with Hollywood.

The studio heads saw TV as a joke.

Their business was making movies.

Had they seen they were in the entertainment business, then they would have embraced the new medium.

Dry-cleaning. Once a huge growth industry, it got hurt and went into decline when synthetic (washable) fibres came along.

Hundreds, maybe thousands, of businesses went to the wall.

But if any of them had looked beyond dry-cleaning to cleaning, they may have started innovating through ultra-sonics.

And they would have been back in growth.

As Levitt noted, there is no such thing as a growth industry. There are only companies that recognize growth opportunities and can capitalize on them.

The point is, if you want to grow you have to innovate.

But if you innovate your way further and further into a niche, you are soon going to become uncompetitive.

Relevance is crucial.

*

Here's another story of a brand that was jolted out of complacency and repositioned itself successfully.

Burger King. Founded in the 1950s, by 2000, Burger King was a basket case business. Grand Metropolitan was glad to get it off their hands, selling it in 2002 to a group of investors led by TPG Capital.

One of the first things the new owners did was to invite a handful of ad agencies to pitch for the advertising account.

Among them was a parvenu agency called Crispin Porter + Bogusky, based in out-of-the-way Florida.

Their pitch was short and to the point.

They had watched how people travelling home to dinner at the end of the working day often stopped to buy a Whopper.

They didn't see it as food. They saw it as a moment of pleasure in an otherwise pretty dreary day.

The meeting went something like this.

CP+B: *What business do you think you're in?*

BK: *The fast-food business.*

CP+B: *Nope. You're in the entertainment business. No one ever bought a burger for its nutritional value. They buy a Whopper because it makes them feel good.*

Buying the strategy that they were in the entertainment business rather than the food industry led to fourteen quarters of growth.

It also led to a steady stream of innovative ideas.

Burger King made and sold computer games featuring their advertising character The King. One Christmas they even sold deodorant that smelled of flame-grilled burger. It was a joke, but every can was purchased.

Today, as the advertising industry struggles to find relevance in the convergence of technology, brands and entertainment, there are some intriguing new players.

CAA, Creative Artists Agency, started out representing A-list actors in Hollywood.

In the 1990s, they began creating the advertising for Coca-Cola.

Remember the polar bears?

From talent agency to ad agency.

This year, CAA has created noted campaigns for Neiman Marcus, Diet Coke, Umpqua Bank and Anheuser-Busch. They have won awards for work for Canada Goose and General Motors.

This is a company offering relevance and reassurance to clients who all recognize that the old model of buying advertising has changed.

However, you don't have to go back all that far in time to see the obverse of this – a business getting its diversification strategy so obviously wrong it very nearly died.

Throughout the 1990s, Saatchi & Saatchi had been the UK's leading advertising agency by a country mile.

They were expanding aggressively and their share price was rocketing. Then they made a bid to acquire the Midland Bank.

The Midland flatly rejected the approach, observing that Saatchi's was completely unqualified to run any sort of financial services business, and the rest, as they say, is history.

The brothers were ridiculed.

The share price plummeted.

Over the next four years, 7,000 employees were reckoned to have lost their jobs in the group.

From jingles and slogans to taking deposits and arranging loans?

A bridge too far.

So, when you stop and ask yourself, what business are we in, really, make sure you also ask what business are we *not* in?

Ideas about making money rather than ideas about spending money

I read somewhere that a research team at Harvard Business School had analysed the minutes from the board meetings of a number of Fortune 100 companies.

Apparently, on average, the boards spent 95 per cent of their time together discussing how they planned to spend their money. Only 5 per cent was spent on how they were actually going to make it.

Here's a thought. Why not do the opposite at your next board meeting? Spend 95 per cent of the meeting discussing how you can make money.

One thing is for sure, you will be opening up the room to ideas.

Which is when interesting things might happen.

When I first encountered Elmwood, the company was a smallish design studio in Leeds.[33]

Now, making money out of design has never been easy because it is a project-based business. Agencies constantly waste time and human resource pitching for clients they don't have at the expense of clients they do.

The Elmwood board met late one afternoon and the subject of how they might make more money was raised.

'How can we make money when we're asleep?' was the provocative question from the chair.

'Oh God,' someone groaned. 'If we're going to be here all night, then I'm going to make myself a cup of tea first. Anyone else want one?'

'A cup of builder's for me, yes thanks,' came a reply.

And from that chance remark came Builder's Tea.

Elmwood sourced the leaves in India, signed import contracts, negotiated the duties payable and learned about the laws that have to be observed when you create any comestible.

Two years later they launched their brand.

Now, it hasn't challenged PG Tips in the market.

But what it has done is allow Elmwood to talk to prospective clients in a completely new way, as one of them.

'So, how did you get distribution into Sainsbury's?'

'Aren't Tesco's buyers tough?'

Elmwood's idea was to experience for themselves what their clients face daily.

The innovation was not a new kind of tea, but a new kind of agency behaviour. Where most agencies are good at dispensing advice, here was one putting its money where its mouths were.

In the ten years since I first visited Elmwood in Leeds, they have opened up in London, New York, Singapore, Hong Kong and Melbourne.

What business are they in?

Design? Or the business of building brands?

What business are *you* in?

How to turn disaster to good account

It was Winston Churchill who offered the advice, 'Never let a good crisis go to waste.'

When everything is ticking over nicely, there appears to be no need for new ideas. It's only when things go wrong, terribly wrong, that ideas are urgently required.

War usually leads to some big ideas.

Many of the technologies of today emerged out of the carnage of World War II.

Navigation systems for 'our' planes; radar systems to detect 'their' planes.

Landing systems to help planes land in the dark.

Incidentally, as further evidence that one innovation often leads to others, the development of radar also led to the microwave cooker.

The V2 rocket was targeted at London but the science behind it helped put Neil Armstrong on the moon.

And, of course, it made the Manhattan Project possible.

This has been the subject of books, TV dramas and films. The race to create a nuclear bomb out of which emerged nuclear power as an alternative method of powering ships and submarines as well as of generating electricity.

Slightly less contentious (not everyone would say splitting the atom was a *good* idea) was the Enigma machine and the shove in the back it gave to computer science.

The spray can was invented to help soldiers in the Philippines combat mosquitoes.

Penicillin, though discovered in 1927, was mass produced and saved untold numbers of troops from septicaemia.

Nylon.

First for parachutes, second for legs.

Aluminium.

Amazingly, aluminium was more valuable than gold.

It was light, it was beautiful but it was incredibly difficult to extract from bauxite ore.

Napoleon III served dinner to his important guests on aluminium. Lesser dignitaries got gold plates.

But in the war, new techniques to extract alumina were developed and the metal became fundamental to the building of aeroplanes and, less glamorous but arguably just as important, mess tins for the troops.

Creativity *in extremis* has provided some of the great stories of modern times.

In fact, the 1995 film *Apollo 13* is used in many corporate training programmes as a model for crisis management.

The original intention had been to put Lovell, Fred Haise and Jack Swigert on the moon.

When an oxygen tank exploded, that put paid to that idea.

Now the task was to try to return to earth in the lunar module, the small part of the spacecraft that was supposed to take them from the command module to the surface of the moon and back again.

The story of how they flew the lunar module, though it had never been designed to be flown, can still raise goosebumps.

The lessons of Apollo 13 are:

- Plan for every possibility. Then plan again.

- Now train your people against those possibilities.

- Ensure there is a clear command structure. That

everyone understands the risks and who makes the decisions when everything goes pear-shaped.

When it's life or death, you'll think of something

Sometimes you have an idea because you *have* to.

The consequences of not cracking the problem are too severe.

Archimedes, for instance. He worked for Hiero, the Tyrant of Syracuse. The word tyrant acquired its modern meaning from him. He was not a personality noted for his warmth and kindness, shall we say. He had been given a golden crown in tribute by some lesser lord. Being of a suspicious nature, he wondered whether the crown had been made entirely with gold or whether he was being conned. Perhaps his new crown was a mix of gold and less expensive silver?

Archimedes was given the task of finding out. Or else he faced execution.

Obviously, he couldn't melt down the crown.

While considering the problem, he ran himself a bath, the way you do when you may not have more than a weekend to live. As he settled himself in the water, he noticed that the further he sank down, the more water spilled over the rim of his tub.

This was when he is reputed to have run out into the street stark naked, shouting 'Eureka'. He had realized that the displaced water was an exact measure of his volume.

So, ingots of silver and gold, though they might weigh precisely the same, would be different in size because gold is heavier than silver.

Next stage was to weigh the crown. Then see how much

water it displaced from a bowl. Then do the same with gold of identical weight. Then silver.

And yes, it turned out Hiero had been cheated. The crown was a fake. But Archimedes kept his head.

A wonderful story of someone becoming creative and inventive because he simply had to be is told in Janet Gleeson's excellent book *The Arcanum*. In 1701, Johann Friedrich Böttger, being young and thoughtless, boasted in the taverns of Dresden that he was close to discovering the philosopher's stone.

In other words, he knew how to turn base metal into gold.

The alchemists of the day were excited by the philosopher's stone because they thought it would reveal the secret of immortality.

Augustus the Strong, Elector of Saxony, was less interested in this aspect of it. He just wanted the gold.

He had declared war on Sweden and needed to pay for his adventures.

He imprisoned Böttger and made him a deal.

Make gold. Or else.

Insanely, Böttger dug an even deeper hole for himself by writing to Augustus and bragging that he could produce 100,000 thalers of gold each month.

A few years earlier, Böttger had studied to be an apothecary. He wasn't a complete fraud. Mostly a fraud but there was a bit of him which understood the principles of experiment and test.

At some stage of his early imprisonment he met the nobleman Ehrenfried Walther von Tschirnhaus. He was the equivalent to the Minister for Trade at the Elector's court.

He had set up glass factories and dyeing plants to make money for Augustus.

What he wanted to do was to make porcelain.

At that time, porcelain was imported from China and was stupefyingly expensive. No one could work out how it was made. One hunch was that it was made from crushed lobster shells. The Chinese weren't saying anything.

The process of combining china clay, kaolin, and pegmatite, a form of granite, was something they intended to keep to themselves.

After meeting Tschirnhaus, Böttger decided that his best hope for survival was to turn from the impossible, making gold, to the possible, making porcelain.

And, by golly, he cracked it.

And out of it came an entire industry.

Innovate or Die is the title of a book by Jack Matson. In Böttger's case, it was a very real threat.

Apple is a company that has so nearly gone belly up. In extremis, Steve Jobs was invited back to the company he had created. There was no warning at all that this Californian maker of desktop computers was about to launch the iPod.

And where did the iPhone come from?

What Jobs did was to understand the regenerative power of innovation. He knew that without brilliant new products Apple would not survive.

His genius was not to look inwards at the company and its competencies, in which case they would have stuck to desktops and laptops, but to look outwards – at people. What they might find useful and desirable.

Then he drove his people ferociously hard to get them to deliver.

*

In the absence of an immediate and pressing danger to your business, the best thing to do is to imagine the worst that could happen and plan for it.

In Chapter 5 (The Creative Toolbox, pages 128–85) we talk about the value of scenario planning.

Forewarned is forearmed, they say.

How to create a creative environment

If you can hire creative people and give them the space in which to have their best ideas, then you can preside over extravagant growth.

To do this, you have to be sympathetic to creativity and to creative people.

You have to see that there is value in establishing and maintaining a creative culture.

How you behave can either inspire your people or discourage them.

Years ago, I worked in a company where there was a relatively young director with huge personal ambitions.

He was made Director of Internal Organization, which we all thought rather funny but which he took very seriously.

So seriously that one Monday morning he walked around the agency at 9.30 a.m. and noted that at least three-quarters of the creative department had yet to arrive.

He sent out an all-staff memo, sniffily reminding everyone that they were employed to work between the hours of 9.30 a.m. and 5.30 p.m.

All the forty art directors and copywriters decided they would do exactly that.

For the next three days they all trooped out on the dot of 5.30 p.m.

In most agencies, that is exactly when the most important meetings happen. The account managers come limping back from client meetings and need to debrief and rebrief.

Within forty-eight hours the previously smooth running of the machine had become juddery and fractious.

Deadlines came and went, promises were broken, relationships strained.

On Thursday, Martin Boase, the chairman, wandered round the creative department, chatting to all and sundry about this and that, adding as an afterthought to each conversation, 'Oh, by the way, there won't be any more memos about time-keeping.'

On Friday morning at 9.30 a.m. most of the creative department was empty.

But it was full at 6 p.m., half-full at 7 p.m. and still not empty at 8 p.m.

The moral of this tale? If you're anal, expect arsey behaviour.

Tell people what to do and they will do only what you told them.

Treat them with regard and you will get their loyalty and their engagement. Netflix, for instance, doesn't have a holiday policy. People take what time off they want, when they want.

No one keeps a record. Apparently, Netflix senior management believe that rules and regulations stifle creativity. They recognize that people do their best work when they aren't filling in time sheets. In return for expectation, they are rewarded with innovation.

Time sheets

One company I know allows its people half an hour a day to complete their time sheets.

What a waste of time!

There's nothing like filling in time sheets to make you feel a slave to the system.

It is proof that creativity has been commoditized.

You buy it in fixed lengths.

It was ever thus.

Michelangelo lay on his back for three years and painted a masterpiece on the ceiling of the Sistine Chapel. He then spent the rest of his life bitching about how his genius was not rewarded properly.

John Ayling is the boss of the UK's most successful independent media agency. He told me he had decided to abandon time sheets.

When his senior executives did their forecasting at the beginning of the year, some of them would overestimate and some of them would underestimate.

It all balanced out in the end.

Abandoning time sheets led to an immediate increase in morale because John's message to his people was basically one of trust.

When you trust your people to do their best for the common good, then they (usually) raise their game.

Shoot the dogs early

There are always going to be people who abuse your trust.

People who are pains. The moaning minnies, the rumour-mongers and the back-stabbers.

If you let poison ivy grow, it strangles the whole tree.

Everyone knows who the troublemakers are.

Get rid of them.

Really, firing unpleasant people is how you make everyone else feel good about themselves.

The Corcoran Group is a large real-estate company on the East Coast of America.

Apparently Barbara Corcoran used to have an annual cull of her poorest performers. She called it 'shooting the dogs early'.[34]

What looked like ruthlessness was actually very supportive of her best people. She would not allow them to be dragged down by the others.

Bill Bernbach grew DDB in the 1950s by hiring from outside the recognized pool of talent of the period, the mid-1950s.

Most ad agencies in the Don Draper years were exceedingly WASP. And exceedingly male.

Not DDB.

But even Bernbach had a guiding principle when it came to hiring. 'No matter how talented they are,' he said, 'life is too short to live with shits.'

It's called the ethylene effect.

It's what happens when one strawberry in the punnet goes mouldy. It produces a natural gas which, among other characteristics, is a ripening agent. It encourages all the other fruit to rot.

How to inspire ideas

As far back as 1909, H. J. Heinz had a suggestion box in the factory.

Theoretically, inviting your workers to contribute to the development and the success of the organization is a good idea.

You just need to be careful how you do it.

How about this from a regional fire service?

Suggestions should be submitted electronically using electronic form FS 902 (for internal use only) located in the Forms section of the Intranet site.

The electronic Form FS 902 should be completed and saved before emailing to your line manager, who will annotate it and forward it via email to the Corporate Services department.

The Line Manager is responsible for determining whether the suggestion falls within the applicant's normal duties.

Where the scope of duties of an employee is not clearly discernible, the following criteria will apply:

— Could the suggestion have been implemented without reference to the Staff Suggestion Scheme?

— Would the contributor be open to criticism for not having made the suggestion part of his/her normal work?

If the answer to either of the above two questions is 'yes', the suggestion will not be eligible for an award.

There are two more pages of this bureaucratic twaddle.

Seriously, how tempted would you be to make a suggestion?

That's not to say the suggestion box is completely useless.

Where the invitation to contribute comes from the very top, you have a culture of openness and fearlessness.

When Lou Gerstner demanded that the elephant should learn to dance, the company was transformed by its middle-ranking employees. Not by the bigwigs.

Gary Hamel, in *Harvard Business Review* (June 2000), tells the story of David Grossman.[35]

During the Winter Olympics of 1994, where IBM was a principal sponsor, he noticed that Sun Microsystems were ripping off all IBM's raw data and serving it on their own website.

He sent the IBM Worldwide Marketing Director a note, informing her that IBM's Olympic feed was being ripped off.

The fudged reply he got made it obvious that no one had a clue what a website was, so Sun Microsystems' theft did not seem to be worth worrying about.

So he got in his car and drove four hours to her office.

There, wearing his programmer's uniform of khakis and open-necked shirt, he set up his workstation to give marketing director Abby Kohnstamm (and anyone else interested) a demo of some early websites.

A senior executive called John Patrick took a look.

He hired Grossman, found a programmer in IBM who knew his stuff and between them they created IBM's first intranet.

Then he wrote a manifesto about the web titled 'Get Connected' and sent it out across the company.

Soon 300 enthusiasts had joined the virtual Get Connected team.

John Patrick broke all IBM's house rules to get the company to take the web seriously and to build their own Olympics site for the 1996 summer games. A suit and a nerd helped transform the company because they *could*.

What you need to understand is that for the creative

people in your company, money is *not* the reward. People who want to make a difference are motivated by the respect (and envy) of their peers. Not by the lure of £1,000.

Psychological safety

A creative culture is one in which there is 'psychological safety'.

In other words, your people don't feel inhibited. They feel secure enough within the group to have ideas and share them. At its simplest, they can be themselves.

Mostly that is because they have seen *you* being human too.

Harvard professor Amy Edmondson defined psychological safety in a 2015 TED talk.

Then Julia Rozovsky at Google ran a project to test the concept within the company. To her amazement she found that the teams comprising the cleverest people did not always produce the best work.

In a lengthy piece in the *New York Times*,[36] journalist Charles Duhigg wrote about her work, concluding that it is apparently more productive and a lot more fun to work in teams where senior managers and middle-rankers are mixed in together; where the conversation leaps from topic to topic; where everyone can have a say; where the meeting tails off into general chit-chat about life, the universe and everything.

As opposed to working in a team where everyone is an achiever; where the expert in any particular field talks at length about the subject; where diversions from the topic are deterred; and where the meeting closes at the agreed time and everyone heads back to their desks.

Duhigg's rhetorical question was, which team would you rather belong to?

His conclusion was that you would do better in the less formal, chattier team – not just because they seem to be more relaxed, but also because the data revealed something fascinating.

In all the successful teams at Google, everyone got to speak for about the same amount of time.

In every meeting, there was a fair distribution of voices.

When everyone got an equal chance to talk, the whole team did well.

How to create a sense of security

Often, when someone gets promoted from the ranks into a management position, he/she thinks the job is to issue instructions.

Would that it were so easy.

The real job is to get people to follow you because they want to. It's not just that you have a sense of direction and purpose but you make them feel you have their best interests at heart. You know them as individuals.

How do you stop talking at your team and start listening to them?

Through team meetings.

Fun events.

Getting behind a charity.

Eddie B. got his team to spend a day raising money for Marie Curie Cancer Care. It wasn't a day they had to take as holiday. The company donated their time.

They just had to find ways of achieving the group target of £X thousand.

They managed it.

Then went and drank far too much far too late into the evening.

Although, you can only do something like that once in a while, of course.

Pecha Kuchas, now there's a way of getting the team together and having a laugh once a week.

Pecha what?

Astrid Klein and Mark Dytham were architects based in Tokyo. They owned a small bar called Super Deluxe, which was struggling to survive.

Legend has it that one evening they invited over a bunch of architect mates. But to make the evening a bit of a laugh, each architect had to deliver a presentation of exactly twenty slides, spending no longer than twenty seconds talking about each.

It was a hit.

So Klein and Dytham began organizing regular Pecha Kucha nights and it wasn't long before Super Deluxe was humming.

Now they run Pecha Kucha evenings in 900 cities and have a large community of followers online.[37]

One team I've worked in used to have a PK every Friday afternoon.

Beers and wine were brought in at 4.30 p.m.

At 4.45 p.m., minor fanfare of trumpets, let the presentations begin.

All finished by 5.15 p.m., when it was considered perfectly acceptable to head for home a little early.

In the first few weeks, people were asked to prepare PKs. Then they began to volunteer and after a month Friday PKs more or less organized themselves.

They were fun for the presenter and fun for the audience.

Both parties knew they only had seven minutes to go through.

The implicit rules are that you can cover a serious topic but you can't be boring.

Also, just twenty seconds for each of your twenty slides means you need to be visual rather than verbal. Or musical rather than vocal.

My colleague Gaston presented the twenty greatest electronic dance music tracks from 2000 to 2016.

The next week, I presented the twenty greatest tracks from 9 June to 12 June 1970 and introduced a group of callow youngsters to Jimi Hendrix, Jim Morrison, Ten Years After, Jethro Tull, ELP – and twenty of the bands that had played the Isle of Wight Festival.

Usually people presented twenty slides about their recent projects.

The presentations were almost always eye-opening. We all learned what everyone else was doing. But even more valuable than that building of mutual respect was the fact that everyone in the team of twenty-five got used to talking in front of their peers without embarrassment.

It gave people the opportunity to get things wrong in public. Then get them right.

It also gave the managers the opportunity to look like complete tits.

If you are the boss and you don't mind playing by the same rules as everyone else, it helps everyone relax.

When you flounder or flop, it gives everyone else permission to do the same.

Monday love-in

Steve P. instigated Monday love-ins with his team.

At 10 a.m., everyone got together in a circle.

Standing up, because though the meeting was designed to be sweet, it also needed to be short.

Ten a.m. because that allowed half an hour for people to be late.

Each person was required to tell the rest of the group about one thing that had recently inspired them. And about one thing they were going to be concentrating on in the week ahead.

Inspiration comes as often from life outside work as it does from events within. What Steve got people to do was to talk about themselves outside the job spec.

They trusted each other to listen sympathetically.

In revealing their emotions to each other, they became a stronger group.

It allowed people to be more open with each other.

For instance, when Simon's name didn't appear in the list of credits for a job that had just gone live, he batted his boss an email.

'My name wasn't there. Is there a reason for this, something I should know?'

'Simon, sorry, shocking oversight.'

A second email went out, detailing Simon's contribution.

In many work groups, Simon might easily have begun brooding.

Oh God, Steve doesn't want me in the team.

It's outrageous. I was pivotal to the success of that project.
Steve is a bloody idiot anyway.
I worked so hard on it too. Late nights, early mornings.
This place really gets on my tits.

None of that happened. Instead, psychological safety meant a simple human error did not lead to emotional carnage.

Simon was able to share something that bothered him without fear of recrimination.

Chill time

Team away-days, off-sites and fun sessions are good *if* you have the culture sorted.

If not, they can make the fissures deeper.

For instance, insisting the team meets up in a bar and then making them pay for their own drinks.

One boss thought he was being the most generous boss on the planet when he took away his entire staff of sixty to the Caribbean for four days.

He wanted to say thank you.

However, he happened to be single.

It didn't occur to him that half the people who worked for him were married or in relationships.

They didn't want to go away for four days. Or, if they did, they didn't want to go away with him.

Then there was the boss who invited everyone to his home in the country for a party on a Saturday evening.

Again, most of his people would rather have been at their homes than at his but, dutifully, they turned up. To find a cash bar.

So.

If you're going to have corporate outings:

- Don't do them once in a blue moon. Make sure they are part of the weft and warp of office life.

- Let other people organize each event. That way it becomes theirs rather than yours. It emancipates them.

- Go with the flow. You may not want to go to a ping-pong basement for an entire evening. Tough. Your team is going to arrange events deliberately to test you.

- Pay the bill without a murmur. Try not to mention it the next day, as if you have been astoundingly generous. They have given you their personal time. The least you can do is fork out for a few drinks.

Five tips to make it safe

In summary, here are five things to bear in mind as you set about building a culture that is supportive and imaginative.

- Recognize your own shortcomings. Let everyone else know you know what they are.

- Set up meetings that are designed to be the beginning of something rather than an end.

- Ask questions.

- Let everyone respond. If anyone is being particularly quiet, ask them questions about the problem from what you know is their perspective. 'So, Gail, you are a producer – what do you think the issues might be if we were to move into production right now?'

- Let people go off-piste. They may take the discussion to a much more interesting place.

Say nope to taupe

A bit of colour never goes amiss. A company I visited in Chicago ran an internal campaign trying to get their senior managers to brighten the offices up a bit.

Say nope to taupe.

The real message was, if the bosses couldn't be bothered to create an interesting environment for their people, why should their people do interesting work?

Wieden+Kennedy in London has tried to give every member of staff a sense of shared ownership of their building. Everyone has a six-inch-by-six-inch portrait of themselves in reception.

The Engine Group has encouraged its employees to put an object, any object, on the shelves in the reception area.

These objects are a talking point internally as well as with visitors.

Tech companies and ad agencies set out to create fun spaces deliberately. As one manager put it: how would you feel about going away for an exotic holiday abroad and being put into a hotel room that was a grey box? No pictures on the walls, only instructions of what to do in case of fire?

Well, why should you feel any differently about your office?

Especially since you spend more time there than you do at home.

Also, as well as giving every worker space in which to work, it does seem to be fundamental to all creative organizations that they have spaces in which people can meet 'by accident'.

Instead of having a tiny galley kitchen with a kettle and

a fridge, why not install a chunky Gaggia coffee-maker in a common room?

Turn your workforce into baristas.

While milling around, they meet and chat.

And ideas occur.

Steve Jobs, when he was at Pixar, insisted the new offices were built with the staff loos in the middle of the central atrium.

It meant people had to schlepp all the way to the lobby whenever they wanted a pee. It also meant they bumped into each other.

Who knows if *Toy Story* only came about because John Lasseter was caught short one day and just happened to see Jeffrey Katzenberg in the lobby, who just happened to suggest Lasseter should watch some old 'buddy' movies?

Well, it's possible.

One last thing. Just as important as all of the above is daylight.

Windows.

It's one of the reasons why old warehouses in London and New York have become home to so many start-up businesses.

4:

HOW TO PUT IN PLACE
A CREATIVE PROCESS

If you want to innovate, then you have to set up a process that will allow you to. Without process the people with ideas will be struggling against the tide.

Yes, right-brained people need left-brained people if they are to do what they do best.

I used to work for an agency where it was generally acknowledged that the system was, there was no system.

There was, however, one overarching principle, which was that the work had to be fantastic.

Meetings would be cancelled.

Clients would tear their hair out.

But when the work did get out of the door, it was almost always outstanding.

In truth, there *was* a system.

Quality was more important than punctuality.

There are three basic stages to the creative process.

1. Inspiration – the phase when you have the idea.

2. Clarification – when you work out what the idea means and you flesh it out.

3. Evaluation – when you cost, prototype and test the idea.

Holding a mirror most faithfully to these three stages is Walt Disney's articulation of the creative process.

Looking back on his career, Walt once said, 'There were actually three different Walts. The dreamer, the realist and the spoiler. You never knew which one was coming to the meeting.'

He must have been fun to work with. He embodied three distinct phases in generating ideas and turning them into reality.

The three Walts gave shape to Disney's culture and processes in the 1960s.

This was when they created a department of imagineers.

They were architects, designers, lighting specialists, electronics engineers and, by golly, even a few writers.

By the late 1960s, this team of oddballs was sufficiently successful for Disney to trademark the word 'imagineering'.

If few imagineers were quite as tri-polar as Walt, then the department itself was structured to move ideas along the three stages from eureka to *kerching!*

To date, Disney Imagineering have 115 patents.

They have brought to life eleven theme parks, four cruise ships and a town. Not to mention a chain of stores.

At one stage, *The Lion King* was the eleventh most valuable brand on the planet, extended into a range of videos featuring the warthog and his meerkat pal, musicals, on-ice extravaganzas and assorted experiences.

However, perhaps the neatest template for the creative process dates back some seventy-five years. It may not be brand spanking new but it works for me.

The creative process

In 1939, James Webb Young wrote what was little more than a pamphlet called *A Technique for Producing Ideas*.[38] It may be a guide to creativity written in a bygone era, but it is still as limpid a description of how the brain works as it is a practical step-by-step guide to both creativity and innovation.

He lists five stages:

1. Gather the raw materials.
2. Digest the material.
3. Make no effort of a direct nature to solve the problem.
4. The a-ha! moment.
5. The cold, grey dawn of the morning after.

If this is how the brain works every time it is tasked with coming up with an idea, it is also how many creative organizations are structured.

Research departments gather the raw data, planning people then look for connections, creative people take on the task and move strategy into execution before the idea is prototyped and tested.

You can either follow these five stages yourself as you look for a way to innovate in your business. Or you can depute different people in the team to each.

So, in more detail, here they are:

1. Gather the facts

It may be a cliché but it is true nevertheless: fail to prepare and you can prepare to fail.

This part is all about preparation, getting yourself so immersed in the problem it starts to become interesting.

— What is the task?

— What is the background?

— What is the problem?

— What is the problem, really?

— What do we want to achieve?

— How will we know when we've succeeded?

— What do we know about the situation/market/ people involved?

— And so on.

Getting the facts sounds as if it ought to be easy.

But it turns out not to be the case.

Every fact has an entourage of other facts attached to it.

What you have to learn to do is ask a whole new batch of questions because what you are looking for is an insight, either into how people really think about your product/ service or how they really use it.

Data is the new oil, they tell us. In fact, there is so much of the stuff they call it big data.

The truth is, what you really want is small data. In other words, big data crunched to reveal a simple human truth.

Here's an example of what I mean:

Hundreds of thousands of people go online to search for information about BMWs.

Lazar looked at the data and it was a blizzard of numbers.

But then he started asking, who are these people? What do they do? Where else do they go when they are online?

It turned out that a lot of people who searched for BMW then went on to look at luxury boutique hotels.

Now there's an interesting connection, which begs an idea.

The whole point about this phase of the creative process is you have to ask a thousand questions. Because suddenly you will find a fact that transforms how you view your problem and your opportunity.

I met the manager of a luxury hotel in Paris.

Make that a *mega*-luxury hotel.

He told me that the cheapest suite they had cost over €2,000 a night and that you could buy an Audi A6 every night for the price of their premium suite.

'You can't have many bookings,' I told him.

'Au contraire,' he told me. 'We are fully booked for the next two years.'

All of this based on the simple fact that the hotel owners had computed that 2 per cent of Western Europeans are now millionaires.

That's eight million people.

What are the odds that ten of them might want accommodation in Paris at any one time?

2. Look for a connection

Webb Young offered what is probably the most elegant definition of an idea when he declared an idea to be nothing more nor less than a new combination of existing elements.

So, it follows that the more facts you have, or the more knowledge you have accumulated, the greater the chance you have of making a new and surprising connection.

This is tough. Because as well as knowing everything there is to know about your business, your category, your market, your competitors, you also have to know a whole load of stuff about things that are utterly irrelevant.

Often, it will be a little nugget from a completely different part of your life that allows you to make the creative leap.

I call to the witness box Brian May, lead guitarist with Queen.

It so happens that May studied astrophysics before making the difficult decision to give it up to be a rock star.

When the band were recording 'We Will Rock You', May's background as a physicist let him create the famous and amazing stomping/clapping sound of a thousand fans. Apparently it's something to do with the distances of sound waves and prime numbers.

Two worlds collided and led to a number one hit.

Incidentally, on the subject of creative people, May is an object lesson in himself. He got himself a PhD in 2007. His thesis? Not 'A quantitative study of the effect of celebrity on consumer behaviour' or 'The effects on the UK political environment of rock 'n' roll ideology' but a dissertation on interplanetary dust.

He is an expert in Victorian stereoscopic photographs and is author of *The Poor Man's Picture Gallery*.

He's also quite a good guitarist.

Turning the kaleidoscope

James Webb Young likens this part of the creative process to playing with a kaleidoscope. You turn the barrel of the instrument so all the little bits of glass fall into new shapes and patterns. Then you turn again. And again.

Apparently, the number of different patterns it's possible to get from a day-to-day kaleidoscope is vast.

The metaphor is plain.

Look at the facts again and again. Then again some more.

Does something suggest itself to you?

This is the stage where all the techniques for generating ideas that are outlined in Chapter 5, The Creative Toolbox, become useful.

Work your way through them all.

1. Draw it.
2. Organize a braindump.
3. Challenge assumptions.
4. Imagine parallel worlds.
5. Think the opposite.
6. Make a wish.
7. Try scenario planning.
8. Have yourself a hack.

As I said earlier, it may well be that you don't have an idea instantly. Be patient. King Gillette (see page 119) took two years, working every day of every week of every month, to have the idea that would one day make kissing a man so much more enjoyable for a woman.

At this stage, beware too the false idea. This is the idea that looks good on the surface but which isn't going to fly.

Perhaps it's been done before.

Perhaps there is a flaw in its construction.

Perhaps there is no real need for it.

The patent office is full of such hopeless dreams.

When you come up with an idea and before you test it by

making a prototype or by putting it in front of a focus group, subject it to intellectual proofing.

Look at your idea through the eyes of a child.

The five whys

Children ask questions constantly as they look for real meaning.

When my son was a toddler, he asked, 'Daddy, why is the sky blue?'

So I started trying to explain atmosphere and the effect of light on air.

Then, 'Daddy, why is the sky black at night?'

Aha. That's because the earth is revolving around the sun so the light that makes the particles of air seem blue disappears with the setting sun.

'Daddy, why does the earth revolve around the sun?'

'Um . . . that's the gravity of the sun pulling us and the moon round and round in what the boffins call their orbits.'

'Daddy, why is there gravity?'

'Oh, give it a rest, Henry, please.'

Suddenly we're talking about the origins of the universe and the meaning of life.

Thinking like a child, though, opens the mind to possibilities.

If you can articulate your idea, then ask why would anyone be interested in it?

By the time you get to the third and fourth why, let alone the fifth, you will have gone beyond the commonplace. You will have a far better understanding of the problem you are trying to solve, that's for sure.

Many years ago, I was trying to help Ford launch what became the Focus. At the time it was wittily called the C130.

In a wood-panelled room out at Ford's HQ in Essex, the marketing director leaned forward and told me, 'The new C130 is amazing.'

First why.

Why is the C130 amazing?

It's amazing because we interviewed over three thousand drivers in one-to-one conversations about what they are looking for in a new car. Three thousand!

Second why.

Why did you interview over three thousand drivers? That's two thousand nine hundred and fifty more than you've ever interviewed before.

Well, if you look at Ford's history, it was pretty much a case of the engineers designing and building a car, then handing over to marketing and saying, off you go, sell it. That simply isn't going to work this time. It's important that this car is a car people really want to drive and enjoy driving.

Third why.

Why this new obsession with driving dynamics?

If you look at the car market, we have new competitors. The Koreans are making pretty good cars, which are affordable. So too the Malaysians. Pretty soon cars from China and from India will be available at prices we won't be able to match. We have to move from the default choice to the preferred choice.

Fourth why.

Why do you need to make the move?

In making a car people want to drive, inevitably we are going to be making a slightly more expensive car. So the new C130 needs to be able to justify its price. It can do this if it's packed with features that surprise and delight. Frankly, there is a lot riding on us getting this right.

Fifth why.

Why is it so important?

Because if we don't get it right, we're out of business.

Whether this is actually true, I don't know but it was said that if the Focus flopped, Ford had plans in place to pull out of Europe. Instead they would concentrate in Europe on the luxury marques they owned at that time: Volvo, Jaguar, Land Rover and Aston Martin.

As it turned out, and in large part thanks to the creativity of Ford designer Richard Parry-Jones, who created a car of almost perfect balance, the Focus was a triumph.

Meanwhile, the five whys helped the marketing team get to a truth about the new model. And when it was launched at the Geneva Motor Show, the Focus was displayed on a small island surrounded by water. To get to it you had to cross a bridge. For Ford, this was symbolic of what they saw as a renewed connection with their customers.

3. Walk away from it

In this part of the creative process, Young wrote that you should make 'no effort of a direct nature'.

Allow the unconscious mind to take over.

While you're off doing other things, the brain still chunters away looking for connections.

One of the most famous ad campaigns in the UK of the last thirty years is the Heineken 'Refreshes the Parts Other Beers Can't Reach' work.

The story goes that copywriter Terry Lovelock had spent eight weeks staring at his typewriter.

Nothing.

His brief was, refreshment.

That was it.

Tell the world that Heineken was refreshing in a way that would be memorable.

Lovelock got more and more desperate. But still the creative juices refused to flow. Eventually he decided that a change of scene might help.

He thought he'd go to Marrakech.

As he was leaving, he bumped into Frank Lowe, the managing director of the agency.

Frank was not known for his cuddly personality.

'Terry,' he said, 'come back with a campaign or don't come back at all.'

One night in Marrakech, Lovelock went to bed at around midnight.

At 3 a.m. he woke up. Sat up. And wrote down a sentence on a notepad. Then fell back into slumber.

In the morning he saw he had written: 'Heineken refreshes the parts other beers can't reach.'

His idea led to literally hundreds of awards. Many other copywriters and art directors profited from it with trophies and career opportunities.

Keith Richards has described how he had gone to bed one night with his guitar.

Okay, not everyone goes to bed with a guitar but Keith was solo at that time.

In the middle of the night, he sat up, pushed play on a cheap cassette recorder he had beside the bed and played an eight-note riff.

When he woke, he was startled to see the cassette in the tape recorder had run to the end. He had no recollection at all of recording what was to become The Rolling Stones' most epic hit, 'Satisfaction'.

What he had on tape was two minutes of rock history and thirty-eight minutes of snoring.

Paul McCartney woke up one morning with the complete tune of 'Yesterday' in his head.

In fact, it was so complete he thought he must have pinched it from someone else.

The point here is that Lovelock, Richards and McCartney had spent their entire lives working for that moment to happen.

It was a summation of all the ideas they had ever had.

James McNeill Whistler, when he sued the critic John Ruskin, was asked how he could charge two hundred guineas for a painting he knocked off in just two days.

'It didn't take two days,' he told the court. 'It took me a lifetime.'

As I wrote in Chapter 2, ideas take time.

In my distant past, I hired people to sit and look at the ceiling or to wander around with their hands in their pockets.

Today I bemoan the bean counters, who like to see people with their heads down and their fingers clattering a keyboard. Their hands may be working but their brains probably aren't.

4. Write something, anything

In Young's canon, this is the 'a-ha moment' when, apparently serendipitously, an idea comes to you out of nowhere.

His point is that you have to have gone through phases one to three for a-ha! to happen.

Thus, Henry Ford was already wondering how he could

build cars ordinary Americans could afford when he saw how the Chicago meat-packers worked.

They had a 'disassembly' line. Carcasses of cows were moved on hooks along a belt. At each work station, an expert in one particular form of butchery did his slicing before moving the carcass on to the next expert.

And so on until there was nothing left on the hook but bones. And even those went off elsewhere to make glue.

For Ford, this was an a-ha! moment.

Could cars be created along the same principle?

It turned out they could, but by reversing the procedure, assembling rather than disassembling.

The production line was born. Naturally, it was copied by others who, with hundreds of little innovations, helped it evolve to become faster, smoother and more reliable.

If Henry Ford had not put in all the hard hours looking and learning about industry and commerce, the a-ha! moment may never have happened.

King Gillette worked even harder to make the serendipitous happen.

Most people would *like* to be rich. Few passionately *want* to be. King Gillette was one of the few.

He knew that to be ridiculously wealthy he needed to invent a product that was low-cost but which met an almost daily need.

But what was that?

He spent two years leafing through the dictionary, waiting for an association to spring to mind.

None did.

Till one day he was walking down a street in his native Chicago and happened to glance in through the open window of a barber's shop.

He saw a man being shaved in the manner of the day, with a cut-throat razor, sharpened daily on a leather strop.

Now, it so happened that the day before he had been in a saw-mill, where he had noticed the semi-circular strips of steel either side of the blade, designed to prevent the woodsman from sawing off his thumbs.

A-ha!

Why couldn't there be similar protective strips either side of a razor blade?

In 1901 he founded the American Safety Razor Company.

Even then it wasn't plain sailing. Only when he reversed logic and gave his razors away did the money start to roll in. From the blades.

Serendipity really only happens in the prepared mind.

I publish a magazine about advertising called *Directory*. Clever marketing people tell me I am an idiot for printing a magazine when we could just publish online.[39]

The reason I love good old-fashioned paper (as well as having a website, of course) is because creative people love it too. And here's why.

When I show the magazine to suits, they always open it at page one. Turn to page two. Close it.

Creative people always open it in the middle and start flicking through the pages. Often, they will pause in the conversation because something has caught their eye. A half-connection is being made.

They are willing the serendipitous.

Being deliberately random.

It's something you can't do online, where every click is a considered move.

It is the accidental nature of the turned page that allows creative people to make sudden and totally unexpected connections.

Writers, artists, engineers, coders, designers, copywriters, they are all living in a permanent state of waiting.

That said, the great American writer Gore Vidal[40] recognized that the a-ha! moment won't come unbidden. You have to coax it.

He said, 'This is when you have to make yourself sit down to write something, anything, even if it's your suicide note.'

If you're in the ideas business and you freeze, you can become paralysed.

Writer's block is a very real spectre.

Don't I know it.

If you remember the Duke Ellington story in Chapter 2, start by taking someone else's idea and adapting it. Playing with it. Turning it upside down. Looking at it with fresh eyes.

Don't get obsessive about originality.

Wanting to do something completely new is admirable. It is also facile. Imitation is not just the sincerest form of flattery, it is a basic principle of evolution. It is how ideas continue to provide value.

The strategist, philosopher, trainer and author Mark Earls has written a delightful treatise on the subject called *Copy, Copy, Copy: How to Do Smarter Marketing by Using Other People's Ideas*.[41]

His theory is that we have evolved to our current state as a species through endless copying. When your mum and dad got it together, their genetic material got copied into you. Or, rather, miscopied because you may be similar to them but you are completely different.

It's the same with ideas. Copy an idea but the context you place it in will mean it invariably mutates into something else.

Kris Pennella copied the Cornish pasties she encountered in the UK and sold them in Portland but cooked to vegetarian and vegan recipes that would have horrified most Cornishmen.

In the 1970s, Western journalists mocked Japanese car makers for copying American car design. But it didn't take long before Japanese cars began making serious inroads on the American market.

Novelty is when you do something new but not necessarily better.

Putting fins on a Cadillac, for example.

You could even argue that the pursuit of novelty is unnatural. Put it this way, whenever novelty occurs in nature, it becomes the stuff of travelling shows.

The bearded lady; the Siamese twins; the elephant man.

Copying, by contrast, is a natural thing to do.

The Beatles weren't the first group of four young men to come together with three guitars and a drum kit.

In fact, in the business world, it is the copyists who often have the greatest success.

The computer mouse was invented by a chap called Douglas Engelbart at Stanford University in 1968.

It was copied and used in early computer experiments at Xerox PARC in the 1970s.

This is where Steve Jobs saw it in 1979.

Understanding at once what this meant for personal

computing, he raced back to Apple and totally changed the direction his designers were taking.

According to Malcolm Gladwell, 'He wanted menus on the screen. He wanted windows. He wanted a mouse. The result was the Macintosh, perhaps the most famous product in the history of Silicon Valley.'[42]

Rocket Internet is a German company which was founded by three brothers.

From the start, their model was to copy successful business models elsewhere – legally.

They took Zappos, a brilliantly innovative online shoe retailer, founded in Las Vegas by Tony Hsieh, and recreated it in Europe as Zalando.

Today, Zalando is valued at $5 billion.

GrubHub is an American food delivery service, founded in 2004. Its success has spawned any number of imitators, among them FoodPanda, founded in 2012 and already operating in twenty-four countries.

I have recently read about a Nigerian venture capitalist who has started an Imitation Fund to encourage start-ups to bring to West Africa ideas that have worked successfully elsewhere.

In summary, in this phase, start work.

Make mistakes and see where those mistakes lead you.

William Perkin was a young chemist, who, in 1856, discovered both the colour mauve and a new dyeing process. He was actually trying to create synthetic quinine to help fight malaria in the further reaches of the empire.

Charles Goodyear created vulcanized rubber by accident when he left a rubber compound on the stove and came back to find it had become tough and durable.

Just by doing something, riffing off an existing idea or even going off at a tangent and exploring an area completely unconnected with your end objective, you are encouraging an a-ha! moment to happen.

5. Test it

An idea isn't an idea until you test it.

That's how Bill Bernbach transformed advertising. He put two people with very different skill sets together, so they could constantly test their ideas on each other.

'How about a rhino riding a bicycle?'

'Don't be a moron.'

For James Webb Young, the testing phase is the most exciting part of the creative process. This is when other people start igniting off your spark.

It is when ideas scale up and new possibilities emerge which no one had predicted.

Today, in the digital world, testing an idea has never been easier.

In *How Google Works*, Eric Schmidt and Jonathan Rosenberg set out their stall by reminding the reader that we are now living at the meeting point of three convergent trends.

One: thanks to the Internet it now costs you nothing to find out about anything.

Two: mobiles put everyone in touch with anyone and everything.

Three: the cloud is making new tools and systems available on inexpensive, pay-as-you-go tariffs.

It means just about every business you can think of is open to business.

Some of these new ideas are shatteringly disruptive.

Uber is a taxi service that owns no cars.

Airbnb is the largest hotel chain in the world without owning a single hotel.

Netflix has turned the concept of television inside out.

These companies have become so successful so rapidly because it is cheap to experiment.

A small team of engineers and designers can take a brief and turn it into a product, then push it out to see what happens. In a few weeks.

Then, if it gets traction, they can scale it up.

Snapchat took Evan Spiegel from the breadline to billionaire in two years.

The fact is, technology now allows you to be quick in this fifth phase. Actually, you *need* to be quick. While you are taking your time, it is almost certain there is someone else out there trying something similar.

Test and learn.

Adapt and evolve.

Fail fast.

Fail better.

The crucial element here is you are now engaging with your potential customers.

When a company starts to occupy itself only with what it does well, it soon slides into irrelevancy.

You have to work hard at what you're not good at. This forces you to look outwards, at people and what they want and what they do, rather than inwards, at your own systems and capabilities.

Perhaps the story of Xerox PARC is a story of incredible institutional failure. It was a creative epicentre.

They invented the personal computer. But didn't know

what to do with it until Gary Starkweather designed the laser printer.

They gave away the idea. Or, at least, they let Steve Jobs get away with it. In sticking to their knitting, which was making and selling printers, they completely missed the big idea.

On the other hand, they did make several billion dollars from knit one, purl one and drop one.

Google continues to innovate by applying the simple rule of 'user first'.

Initially, Google Maps had no obvious financial worth. It was simply a hell of a great way of helping people explore the world and navigate their routes around it.

Once Maps was up and running, people began to discover ways to make a few bob from it.

Sir Frank Lowe once said he was in the business of making advertising, from which he made money.[43]

He was not in the business of making money by making advertising.

There is a big difference.

Creative people are seldom driven by money. They may end up with lots of it but that is not the purpose.

They do what they do because they have an inner compulsion. They know that money follows those who are makers.

When to stop

Perhaps there is a sixth phase, which is to know when you're done.

In creativity workshops, we sometimes get people to tell one-word stories. You start a sentence off with the word 'When . . .' The person next to you takes it up. 'Animals . . .'

The next person adds 'Get . . .' The fourth contributes 'Hungry . . .' And so on.

After about thirty words the sentence has collapsed into meaninglessness.

When animals get hungry they go into town and they sit and look in windows and then they go back to the forests and lie down until it is time to go shopping but they can't so they start roaring . . .

The trick is to get attendees to know when to finish the sentence so it *is* a story. Knowing when to wind up is a skill in itself.

When Edison was told he had failed to work out how to make his lightbulb work, he made his famous reply: 'On the contrary, I have succeeded in identifying a thousand minerals which will not work.'

Seth Godin has identified 'dips' and 'cul-de-sacs'.

A dip is when you just can't see where you're going but if you do get over that hump, you're going to be the best in the world.

A cul-de-sac is when you just wind up again and again at the same spot.

You can usually spot a cul-de-sac when your shoulders sag at the very thought of returning to the project.

When you start getting heart palpitations because you are working late every night and drinking too much coffee.

When you've spent not just all your money but all your energy on the project.

Walk away.

Start something else.

If you don't unstick yourself, you will come unstuck.

Sometimes bravery is knowing you've come to a dead end.

5:

THE CREATIVE TOOLBOX

This chapter is called The Creative Toolbox because it contains a number of different ways you can arrive at an idea.

Bear in mind, idea and execution are not the same.

I have an exercise I do in my workshops.

Execs are asked to choose two words at random.

Not words that are related to each other, like ham and eggs or glass and water.

Random words like 'peach' and 'car'.

These were the two words Mandy jotted down.

Next I ask attendees to spend five minutes trying to create a new product or service from their words.

Mandy came up with the idea of windscreens for cars which have reactive glass. The top strip of the windscreen would go darker the sunnier it got, like reactive sunglasses.

It would make driving safer.

Usually, when people present their ideas back to the group there is laughter at how daft, useless or impossible the ideas are.

This time, when Mandy explained her idea, the room went 'oooh!'

It was an idea that solved a problem.

Met a need.

No one had seen it before.

It was an idea everyone could see made sense and had value.

Now all Mandy had to do was put together a presentation.

She would have to go to talk to as many venture capitalists, business angels and banks as would see her.

She would need to raise £200,000 or thereabouts to do a feasibility study, find a glass company to build a prototype, test it and patent it. Then she could start approaching car companies.

If one or two liked the idea, then she would need a whole lot more funding to build a factory, hire the labour, sort out a distribution system and everything else.

On the whole, Mandy thought she'd rather stay a junior marketer working for a telco.

Jacob B. is one of the most creative people I have ever met. He streams out ideas daily.

They almost always start with, 'Have you ever wondered . . .'

For instance, in Denmark car tax is at 100 per cent of the purchase price of the vehicle. So a big, fashionable 4×4 costs a big, ridiculous amount of money.

Except that they can be classified as agricultural vehicles provided the owners take out the back seats.

A lot of Danes chose to do this.

Turning a big Beemer or Land Rover into a two-seater was a fashion statement, a status symbol.

We were talking about this one day and Jacob started off, 'Have you ever wondered what they do with the back seats when they take them out?'

He rang his local BMW dealer.

'Why are you asking?'

'Well, I thought I might sell them to students or ad agencies as cheap sofas. They look trendy, they're leather.'

'Oh, would you?' The voice the other end was almost pleading. 'BMW in Germany won't take the seats out at the factory, they make us do it. I have a container behind the showroom just packed with seats.'

Did Jacob do it?

No.

Too much work.

He is very clear about it. He lives to play tennis. Not to spend his time rushing around doing deals, looking for retail outlets.

He wants to be comfortable, he doesn't want wealth. It will take too much managing.

Idea and execution are not the same.

Remember Edison's words: 'Creativity is 1 per cent inspiration and 99 per cent perspiration.'

So, the first question to ask is: are you prepared to have an idea?

Are you up for the hard work it entails?

Peter J. is a young designer who had an idea about how companies could better manage their vendors and contractors.

In the eighteen months since he threw the towel in on his job to go it alone, he has had precious little life in his life.

At one stage, he looked older than me.

He has raised £3 million so far and is now concentrating on proofing the idea.

It has to work superlatively in one domain before he can start scaling it up.

The money has gone on opening offices in New York and San Francisco as well as in London.

He has hired fifteen people so far.

His investors look at everything he does. No business class travel for PJ.

It's quite possible he won't make any money at all until he sells a controlling interest to someone else, which is when all the fun may fade.

The creative process here has been a creative leap followed by endless testing and improvement of the product.

Endless.

It helps that he is young and single.

1. Draw it

'If a picture isn't worth a thousand words,
then the hell with it.'
Ad Renhardt

Left-brain thinking means that most people tend to write sentences when they are thinking. They express their ideas as verbal constructs.

This is when you only have half a mind to solve the problem, literally.

So, trying to get people to visualize and draw the end goal is a deliberate way of stirring up the right hemisphere.

Where do you want to get to?

What is the vision?

Sketch it.

Half thirteen

Here's a little exercise for you.

What is half thirteen?

When I ask a group this question, the answer is immediate.

Six and a half. Or six point five, if you like.

Then I ask the question again.

What is half thirteen?

Silence.

'What is half thirteen?'

'Six point five.'

Now I ask people to write 13 on a piece of paper.

'Aha, half thirteen is one.'

'Half thirteen is three.'

'Half thirteen is thir.'

'Half thirteen is teen.'

Depending how you draw your threes, half thirteen could be seventeen.

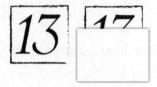

It could look a bit like the Loch Ness monster.

And who says it has to be written in our own number system? Write it in Roman numerals and now half thirteen is eleven. Or two.

XIII

This may be just a brainteaser but it offers two valuable learnings.

One, trust the evidence of your eyes.

Two, there is never just one answer to the problem.

Draw a picture of yourself, aged 10

In my workshops I sometimes get people to draw pictures. I ask them to draw a picture of themselves aged ten.

If you have ten minutes, get a piece of paper and give it a go.

Several things happen.

Firstly, you have to use your imagination to remember what you were like at that age.

Secondly, you have to have an idea about yourself.

Now, most people will draw photographically. In other words, they capture a still image, which requires a narrative in which they explain what they were up to at the time.

A lot of men draw pictures of themselves in football strip.

A lot of women draw themselves in tutus.

Some people, however, think symbolically.

One guy drew a simple bird-flying squiggle.

When he was ten, he said, he was as free as a bird. Since then, life had been a series of entrapments.

A champion swimmer drew a picture of a crown. She said it was because her dad had told her that one day she would be the queen of the pool.

Thirdly, and this is rare, you may have an idea which breaks the rules.

This is wilful creativity.

Sure, you know what the brief is.

You know what everyone else will do.

Maybe you can be a bit clever? Maybe you can make a

statement about yourself? You *want* to be different. You deliberately set about doing the unobvious.

For instance, Chris was the first person in any of my workshops ever who, seemingly, chose not to engage with this exercise.

'I'm sorry you don't want to do a drawing,' I said.

'Oh no, I am taking part,' he replied.

So, after ten minutes, I asked everyone to show their drawings and talk about them.

It came to Chris.

He held up a blank sheet of paper.

'When I was ten,' he said, 'I was never there. I was in care. I kept running away from all the foster homes I was sent to. So wherever I was meant to be, I was absent.'

My guess is that everyone in that workshop remembers Chris and his story.

So, have a look at your drawing.

Is it a snapshot?

Is it symbolic?

Or is it provocative?

Whatever you've drawn, you've been using a part of your brain that's been lying dormant since art class when you were, well . . . ten.

Here's another drawing exercise to use that right hemisphere.

If there is a group in the room, draw a squiggle on a piece of paper. Now hand it to the person on your left.

Look at the squiggle and turn it into a picture of something recognizable.

Zig-zags become a dinosaur.

The big loop in a scribble suddenly becomes a nose.

What's the point?

Why do these silly exercises?

Because they get people laughing. And, for me, laughter is the sound of people having and sharing ideas with each other.

Also, they get people thinking differently. Warmed up for the next drawing exercise:

Draw the problem

One of our clients had asked us for a new campaign.

The planner had been struggling to find any point of difference between this particular insurance company and any other.

Mostly because there wasn't one.

She brought me the creative brief, which was a meandering page of hopelessness.

So I tried this technique on her.

'Draw me the problem, Karen, please.'

She picked up a pen. 'That's easy.'

This what she drew.

'Okay, so what is that?'

'The financial services market is just so complicated. No one has a clue what any of the products are or what the various claims mean. What the heck is APR? What is AER when it's at home? Know what your PSA is? What's a PEP, what's an ISA? Remember TESSAs? It's all a mess.'

'So draw the solution.'

She drew a single straight line.

'What's that?'

'It's communications that are so straightforward, we won't need to put all the legalese at the bottom of it.'

'Now that sounds like a pretty exciting brief to me.'

A few months later the team launched a series of ads, booklets and brochures all modelled on the Ladybird books of our childhood.

I worked for a while with Greenpeace, trying to find a solution to the problem of how the Common Fisheries Policy worked in the European Union.

I ran several workshops, one at the Cannes Festival of Creativity.

Fishing quotas had been reassigned so that small-time fishermen, father and son businesses, only got 20 per cent of the annual allowance even though they accounted for 80 per cent of the total fishing fleet.

Giving 80 per cent of the quota to a handful of large operators was supposed to help solve the problem of dwindling fish stocks.

It did the opposite.

In trying to define the exact problem we needed to solve, one of the women in the group drew a big, black square.

'It's the sea,' she explained. 'No one can actually see

beneath the surface of it. So we assume that there are loads of fish left.'

One of the ideas that emerged from this was to take the film *Finding Nemo* and remove all the fish from it. So Nemo would swim in an empty sea for all ninety minutes.

Okay, so the next problem would be to get Disney to agree to this.

That said, I think I did read that someone in Spain was actually trying to do exactly this.

Perhaps he had come to one of the workshops.

Draw a Mind Map

Mind Mapping was invented by Tony Buzan in the 1960s.

Rediscovered, perhaps.

Porphyry of Tyros is said to have used something like it to chronicle Aristotle's thinking.

Leonard da Vinci is said to have used a similar technique when he was working.

Buzan himself is an interesting fellow.

Not just the man behind Mind Mapping, which millions of people now practise, but the force behind the Mind Sports Olympics, the Brain Trust and a number of other organizations that celebrate the workings of the mind.

He has written many books and he has a website, www. tonybuzan.com. Here he spells out the principles of mind mapping and gives plenty of examples.

You can also buy his app, iMindMap.

In essence, this is what you do:

- Take a piece of paper and lay it out in front of you in landscape rather than portrait form. When I have been working on my annual plans for my little publishing business, I have preferred A3 to A4 because it gives scope to keep extending outwards if a new line of enquiry suggests itself.

- Start in the middle with an image of your starter idea or your goal. I remember when times were tough and my number one priority was paying the school fees, I started with a carefully drawn picture of a treasure chest. The sort of drawing you'd see on pirate maps! Now the mental task was to work out how to fill it.

- Have lots of coloured pens to hand. Colours don't just brighten up the page, they illuminate your mind too. Taking time and trouble to add colour to a particular word or drawing helps print the thought on the wrinkles of the cerebellum. If you can draw images, they tend to be stickier in the mind than words. (Left-brain, right-brain theory again!)

- Start drawing branches out from the centre. Each of these is a train of thought. If you take my panicky map of how to survive, the first branch I drew was to represent the training workshops I ran. What new courses could I offer? Make the branches and the twigs that sprout from them curvy rather than straight. It looks nicer and, as Buzan says, the brain doesn't think in straight lines.

- Stick to one key word per branch. Otherwise you lose focus very quickly. Not Music & Drama but Music. And Drama. Or in my case, not Writing Books but Writing. That allowed me to start thinking about writing a blog. Writing booklets to accompany my courses. Writing a magazine.

The completed map does you two favours.

Firstly, it has forced you to pursue a thought all the way through to the end.

Secondly, you see the bigger picture, literally. Stuff you might have forgotten about re-emerges and now you can start to make a whole new series of interesting connections.

If you look at the very last words on each branch, are there ways and places they can connect?

Put them together and what happens?

One of my branches was named Clients.

This branched out further on into Friends.

And the names of several good mates from university days one of whom just happened to be the CEO of a large financial institution.

It had never occurred to me before that friends could become clients. I dropped him a note, enclosing a brochure and landed a contract.

Linear thinking would never have got me to that idea.

Instead, my pattern of thinking was disrupted by creating a new pattern.

I'm not alone in trying to make my Mind Maps aesthetically pleasing. Some you can see online are works of art.

Authors have used Mind Maps to generate ideas for stories.

The vicar has used them to write his sermons.

An explorer I have heard of has used them to plan his trips to remote parts.

Some people have turned their CVs into Mind Maps.

Paul Foreman has created a Mind Map to show how to draw a Mind Map at http://www.mindmapinspiration.com/

Talking walls

Mind mapping doesn't have to be solitary.

You can do it in groups.

That said, the group needs to be relatively tight, no more than six of you, I'd suggest.

You need a bumper-pack of Post-its because you'll get through a lot of them.

Write the core idea or the ambition on a Post-it and stick it on the wall. Keep it to a single word.

Ideally, you're in a room of decent size so you have a proper wall to work on.

Now invite each person to write a word that spins out from the central thought.

Step back.

Look.

Think.

Now invite everyone to start adding Post-its around those secondary words, spinning them out in a chain if they are developments, clustering them closely if they are interpretations.

If you can use different coloured stickies for each branch, it looks more fun.

After twenty minutes, pause. Look again and start to see if there are new connections to be made, which unlock the problem and suggest an idea.

Use your eyes

As much as anything, the next few paragraphs are a plea to *look* at the world around you. God, as they say, is in the detail.

Graham Greene wrote a short story about a couple having dinner in a London restaurant.[44] The girl is explaining how the sales of her first book mean a future of financial security. Her fiancé is not so sure.

As she talks, he notices the small party of Japanese who come into the place. He notices their studied courtesy. She doesn't notice them at all.

Greene is suggesting that the novelist's job is to be observant.

In the business world, the ability to see things as they are is also a boon.

For instance, when Formule1 hotels were founded in France in the 1990s, there was no actual need for more hotel rooms.

However, the founder believed he had seen an opportunity.

Sitting in hotel lobbies, he noticed how wasteful they are of space.

Also, how costly a lobby is. It has to have staff behind the desk.

Also, most hotels had a bar, which was usually empty.

It too needed staff.

What many business travellers want is to get to a hotel and go straight to their rooms. They don't need a reception area, they don't want a large bar.

Formule1 did away with all that.

Today, you check in online. You get a code, which lets you into your room.

Vending machines provide you with the basics of food and drink.

You sleep, you get on your way.

I heard about a fish farmer, who also had a startlingly effective idea as a result of watching his fish.

Farmed salmon don't command as high a price as wild salmon. The meat is softer. That's because a salmon in a pond doesn't have to swim as vigorously as a wild fish out at sea.

Watching his salmon as they twisted and turned slowly and elegantly in the water, the farmer wondered what would make them swim more energetically.

Answer. A shark.

He dropped a predator in his ponds.

What he lost to the shark he more than made up in the increased price he was able to charge.

It works in reverse as well.

Your customers have eyes too.

In the luxury goods market, how the product looks distinctive is critical.

Louis Vuitton bags and luggage are deliberately obvious. They signal aspiration and worldliness.

Christian Louboutin shoes all have a red sole so everyone else can see that the girl in their heels is both discerning and successful.

Dyson's cyclone cleaners had superior technology to the old sucking Hoovers but what made people buy them were their bright colours and the transparent cyclone barrel.

Up until that moment, all vacuum cleaners were dowdy. Suddenly, here was a machine that was cheerful.

Dyson suggested that cleaning the house was as much of a chore as you made it.

Draw a big cross

Another little exercise about how ideas occur to you when you can see the evidence on paper rather than hold it in your mind.

Draw a cross.

Great.

You have drawn a Cartesian co-ordinate graph.

The horizontal line is your *x* axis, the vertical your *y* axis.

Now you have the beginnings of a map on which you can locate your product or service and where you can also position your competitors.

Depending on what business you're in, how you mark each of the North, South, East and West points is going to be key.

Each axis needs to be able to measure the attributes that potential and actual customers apply to your products and your competitors.

So, here's a very basic map of the smartphone market.

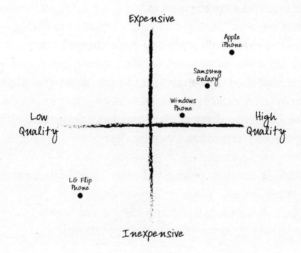

At a glance you can see there is a gaping hole in the bottom right quadrant.

Is there an opportunity for someone to make a phone that does a bit less than the Samsung S7 or the iPhone 6?

That costs less?

Which doesn't catch fire?

In Japan, one mobile phone manufacturer makes a mobile that only makes phone calls.

And guess what? It's a big success. Especially with older people, who also appreciate the larger, easier to tap numbers.

It's right-brained, this map-drawing thing. But it lets you see at a glance where the gaps are.

Literally.

Adam Lury, a splendidly contrarian thinker, was asked to take a look at Red Mountain.

The coffee brand had done well but, in a crowded market dominated by Nescafe, sales were off the boil.

Adam drew a chart and plotted the positions for all the coffee brands he could think of.

They were all clustered together around sociability.

Get together over a coffee to make things happen.

So he went to a diametrically opposite position and argued that Red Mountain should be about the caffeine hit.

Not a drink to share at elevenses but a drink to keep you going through the night.

Opposite is another perceptual map I grabbed at random from the Internet.

When you look at it, do any ideas occur to you?

Expensive/Quick looks like an opportunity.

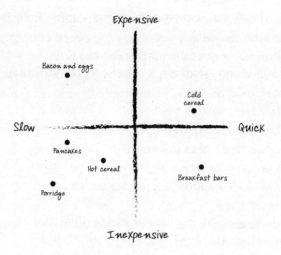

Breakfasts positioned

You set up a breakfast delivery service. Hot breakfasts delivered to executives' desks.

In partnership with Uber.

If other businessmen are anything like me, even if I can afford to spend twenty minutes in the restaurant in the morning having breakfast, I don't feel I can.

I want to get moving.

Feel as if I'm making waves.

For people like me, breakfast in a box.

I climb into the cab, the doorman hands me the box. I eat as I travel to the airport, meeting, office.

I'm not suggesting either of those is viable.

I am suggesting that the moment you show someone a problem, they start finding solutions.

The key word there is 'show'.

*

In *Visual Explanations*, Edward R. Tufte tells the story of how Dr John Snow mapped every incidence of cholera in London throughout the epidemic of 1854.

What he could see was that they were all centred around the water pump on Broad Street (now Broadwick Street) in Soho.

Within twenty-four hours, the pump had been dug up.

Evidence was found of a cess pit leaking sewage straight into the water supply.

Deaths ceased almost immediately.

Up until that moment, it was generally thought that cholera was an airborne vapour that oozed up from the cemeteries and burial grounds of the city.

Now that Snow had established a causal link between the water supply and cholera, tackling the problem was relatively easy.

If you can see clearly, you can think clearly.

Visualize the data

As data has become more and more important to businesses of all shapes and sizes, how the data is shared has led to some radical reappraisals.

The British Library's 'Beautiful Science' exhibition in 2014 showed, among other things, Florence Nightingale's 'rose diagram' of military mortalities in the Crimean War.[45]

When the conflict had come to an end and she had returned home, she was able to show the Royal Commission at a glance that ten times more deaths had occurred from sickness than from battle wounds.

As a soldier, you were safer facing the Russian guns than you were in hospital.

When she started trying to raise funds for a nursing school, the money poured in. People could see the need they were meeting.

David McCandless is an author, information designer and the brains behind the website 'Information Is Beautiful'.

His schtick is simple.

When you visualize data, it allows you to see things and make connections you had never made before.

In his TED talk on YouTube[46] he shows this:

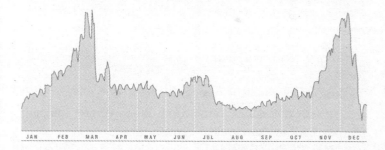

The peaks are at Easter and two weeks before Christmas. The mini-peaks are every Monday. It flattens out over the summer.

So, what's going on?

Someone in the audience suggests that those are the occasions when people go online searching for chocolate.

In fact, it turns out to be data taken from Facebook, recording when some 10,000 couples broke up over the course of a year.

The data reveals that spring is most definitely a time of out with the old and in with the new.

The deepest trough is Christmas Day.

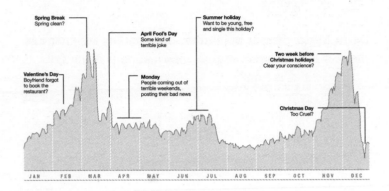

Peak Break-up Times
According to Facebook status updates

Spring Break
Spring clean?

Summer holiday
Want to be young, free
and single this holiday?

April Fool's Day
Some kind of
terrible joke

**Two week before
Christmas holidays**
Clear your conscience?

Valentine's Day
Boyfriend forgot
to book the
restaurant?

Monday
People coming out of
terrible weekends,
posting their bad news

Christmas Day
Too Cruel?

JAN   FEB   MAR   APR   MAY   JUN   JUL   AUG   SEP   OCT   NOV   DEC

No one can bring themselves to break up on December 25th.

Now, when I look at that and I think of chocolate, well – there's an immediate connection. When you're dumped, you buy Cadbury's in industrial quantities.

Firstly, Cadbury should be advertising at these times.

More to the point, there must be opportunities for them to reach dumpees in social media at these peak dumping times.

I would certainly start looking.

Try looking at the data you have in different ways.

Sometimes, visualizing it in blocks or bubbles throws up insights you could not have arrived at by looking at a spreadsheet.

Some of the online tools to help you do this include:

— Exhibit, developed by MIT and an open-source software.

— Visual.ly lets you create your own infographics.

— Tableau is another free visualization service you can find online.

— Google Trends is a brilliant way of looking at data in surprising ways.

These are simple graphs of how often people search for various subjects.

What makes it a fascinating tool is you can compare and contrast topics.

For instance, I have just had a quick look at teenager sports.

Interesting that parkour has been more interesting to more people in the last year than skateboarding and snowboarding.

Maybe there's a business to be had in parkour?

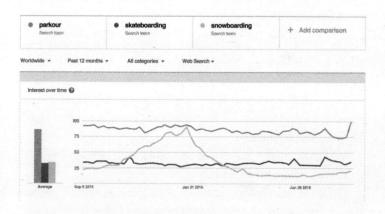

It has none of the rules of football or cricket. It's about finding space and playing in it.

Sounds like a sport for the creatively-minded.

2. Organize a braindump

*'When you have a group of people in a room,
you have the lightbulb. But yours is the finger
on the switch.'*
(Anon)

If the previous chapter gave you some suggestions about how to have ideas when you're on your own, the suggestions from now on in involve working in a group.

Brainstorming, in fact.

This was pioneered by the O in ad agency BBDO, Alex Osborne.

He organized the creative process into three stages.

1. Inspiration

2. Clarification

3. Evaluation

He noticed that people often tended to be destructive of other people's ideas. They would edit their own with equal ruthlessness.

How often have you been in a meeting and someone has piped up, 'Ah! I know . . .' then slumped back in his/her seat? 'No, no, stupid idea.'

You don't know if it was a stupid idea or not.

It was never given an airing.

Osborne set out to establish a process in which people give utterance to all the ideas that popped into their heads, freely and without fear of being ridiculed.

He called it brainstorming.

These days, brainstorming gets a pretty bad rap.

Partly because some people think the word itself is insensitive. Partly because others think sitting in a room and spewing out thoughts in free association is not time well spent.

Personally, I think a good braindump can be stimulating, fun and, usually, rewarding.

The fact is, if you have a problem that needs a solution, you can often be too close to it to find the way through.

Your expertise gets in the way. It's why outsiders can help you find the way in. They don't know as much as you do.

That said, there are some rules.

The first is, you have to have an open mind.

You need to believe that there *will be* a solution.

You have to put aside all your expertise and ask people who know little of the detail to help.

You may find this uncomfortable.

On the other hand, you may also find it inspiring to have your convictions challenged and even disproved.

The second thing is, there has to be a facilitator.

The fine art of facilitation

- The facilitator needs to be creative enough in himself/herself to be able to recognize an idea and encourage further development of it in the session.

- The facilitator probably needs to have enough seniority to command respect. That's because he/she is bringing energy and noise into the room. Wee timorous beasties will watch their session collapse into argument and disarray.

- The facilitator has to make sure every person is

encouraged to contribute. The shy ones can have as much, or more, to offer than the loud, self-confident folk.

- Criticism and sarcasm have to be swiftly knocked on the head. One way of doing this is agreeing upfront to a Penalty Corner. If someone is at all negative, they have to get up, go to the corner of the room, and return.

In addition to having these characteristics, the facilitator has some very specific tasks:

- Plan the braindump. That means finding a room, making sure it has plenty of blank sheets of paper, Post-its, flipcharts and marker pens.

- Sketch out an agenda.

- How long should it last? Some manuals suggest you need four hours for a good braindump. Personally, I think you'd be braindead by then. Trying to have ideas is knackering. It was Robert Frost who once wrote, 'The brain is a remarkable organism. It starts work the moment you wake up in the morning and doesn't stop until you get into the office.' Most of us just go through the motions each day. Active thinking is hard work.

- Your agenda needs to define:
  WHY you have come together.
  WHAT the problem is.
  WHAT you would like to achieve.
  HOW you will know you have achieved it.

- Send out invitations. Eight people is about right. Any more than that and the wallflowers will be able to hide for most of the session. This is a pity because wallflowers are as capable of an amazing insight as an ebullient extrovert.

In the meeting itself:

- Give an indication of how you want to use the time you have.

    Ten per cent of the time should be spent on the set-up.

    Fifty per cent generating ideas.

    Twenty-five per cent discussing the ideas and voting.

    Fifteen per cent on actions going forwards.

- Provide enough background material to stimulate the imagination but not so much that everyone gets bogged down in detail.

- If you are senior within the organization, you have to leave status outside.

    Make clear the room is full of equals.

    I was once invited to a braindump by a corporation bigwig.

    He strode into the room.

    'Right, you lot, I have had a brilliant idea and I want you to help me make it absolutely watertight.'

    After half an hour of not a lot he left the room, slamming the door behind him.

    Try to make people feel that their ideas are valued.

Also, that they might profit in some way from a successful outcome.

Let them know there's something in it for them.

- Make it clear that you have to generate dozens, if not hundreds, of dull ideas in order to get to one that shines.

As the facilitator, you have to be positively neutral. You must write *everything* down on the flipchart.

If someone has a naff, irresponsible or even provocative idea, you capture it.

Not capturing it implies criticism. You didn't think the idea worth anything. Worse, you didn't think the person who offered it has anything useful to say.

There is always someone who wants to test the boundaries. Someone who, frankly, is a bit of a prat.

Prats are waiting to be challenged. So don't challenge them. Write down their dopy suggestions as assiduously as you write down the ideas you secretly think are interesting.

The interesting thing about prats is, if you can avoid rolling your eyes or tutting and take them at face value, they stop being prattish pretty rapidly. And, in my experience, they will then become enthusiastic participants.

Quite often, you'll have a critic in the room.

Critics are people who think they are demonstrating how clever they are when they rip an idea to shreds.

It's easier to pull something apart than it is to build it.

(As a boy, I remember spending days assembling balsawood model planes, even more time putting tissue paper on the wings and applying turps, all of which a bully could smash in a couple of seconds.)

So, try to set Happy Rules.

Ban all 'Buts'. Bonus points for every 'Yes, and . . .'

I usually allow two hours for a braindump.

Fifteen minutes to establish the ground rules and present the necessary information. Then an hour max for the ideas.

After sixty minutes, your brains will all be flagging.

Let them take a break.

Five minutes of fresh air, swinging the arms, getting the blood zipping round a few arteries.

After inspiration, clarification and evaluation

Now start looking at all the ideas that have been captured.

Which ones do people want to talk about?

Why are they talking about those ideas and not the obviously more sensible ones?

How could the idea be developed?

What else does the idea suggest?

If someone has had a particularly arresting idea, get them to explain what they were thinking of, why they made that connection.

Encourage debate.

The trick is to ask questions.

Loads of them.

Open questions.

Remember Rudyard Kipling. In 'The Elephant's Child' he wrote:

> I keep six honest serving men,
> They taught me all I know.

Their names are What and Why and When
And How and Where and Who.[47]

Open questions demand a response. The person you are quizzing has to think.

And what they think could be the beginnings of an idea that will lead to an innovation.

After about thirty minutes of discussion, ask people to vote.

Give everyone three stickers to place against the three ideas they like most.

Or adopt a points system.

Every person can give three points to their favourite idea, two to their second favourite, one to their third.

Then count them up.

Look at the winners.

Now you have to evaluate whether there is any mileage in continuing to work with the top ideas. Or not.

Don't be disappointed if your braindump hasn't led to a stunning new idea or to any sort of solution.

No one said this would be easy.

What you have to do now is reframe the problem.

Send out invitations.

Then braindump again, using two or three or more of the techniques below.

3. Challenge assumptions

Bertrand Russell wrote, 'In all affairs, it is a healthy thing to hang a question mark on the things you have long taken for granted.'[48]

The trouble is, if you are trying to solve a problem, it may well be that the things you take for granted are obscuring the solution.

That's why this technique often works well in brain-dumps.

Simply identifying your assumptions becomes fascinating in itself.

There is *so much* that you don't actually think about. You have just become accepting of it.

For example, I used to assume I needed a job.

But when I lost my job (oh, all right then, when, more accurately, I got fired) I decided I didn't want a job ever again.

So I worked my nuts off and managed to turn my passion into an income.

Creativity paid the mortgage. In devising and running workshops of one sort or another and in having a good rant at conferences and seminars, I earned a living.

Assumptions can be the shackles that are holding you back from making the leap forwards.

The trouble is, you grow so used to wearing those shackles, you become unaware that you're hobbling.

Listing them is a way of bringing to your conscious mind many of your unconscious thoughts.

Simply collecting them on a flipchart if you are working with a group, or on a piece of paper if you are on your own, can be liberating.

Here are ten questions to ask once you've captured an assumption.

1. Who says?

2. Why did we think that in the first place?

3. What proof is there that that's what our customers are buying?

4. Who else is doing what we do and saying what we say?

5. What happens if we stop doing it?

6. What else would we do instead?

7. Who would we need to bring on board?

8. Why do we assume it will be difficult or painful to change?

9. What other assumptions does challenging this assumption reveal?

10. What would be the unthinkable thing to do right now?

I was working with an advertising consultancy not so long ago.

The very first assumption the managers captured on the whiteboard was: We exist to sell our clients' branded products.

Using the ten questions led to a complete repositioning of the consultancy.

1. Who says?
    Er . . . I suppose we do.

2. Why did we think we are in the business of selling media?

    Um . . . well, the media owners tell us we are.

3. What proof is there that's what our customers are buying?

    Now you mention it, what they really value is the data we bring to the party.

4. Who else is doing what we do?

    Pretty much every other advertising consultancy.

5. What happens if we stop doing it?

    No one would notice.

6. What else would we do instead?

    We should be talking about how data leads to insights. And it's those insights that drive everything.

And so on.

The consultancy team made a discovery about themselves. Their customers were buying insights.

But those insights were to do with human behaviour rather than data capture.

As one of the team said, in almost every meeting they were able to tell a chief marketing officer something about her brand or her customer she didn't know.

It made them magicians.

Now, magic is often misused as a word to imply supernatural powers. But listen to someone like David Copperfield and you realize swiftly he is talking about human nature rather than about show business.

He knows how to divert attention so that when he pulls the rabbit out of the hat, literally, it is amazing.

It isn't sorcery. It is science.

In redefining themselves as magicians, the team began trying to build in deliberate 'alakazam' moments to their presentations. It certainly made meetings more fun.

What the ten questions do is force you to validate your unspoken understandings.

If you can come up with a good 'because' for each of them, then you're on firm ground.

Clinging to the wreckage

However, if you make no effort to challenge your assumptions, then you must surely run the risk of becoming set in your ways. Rigid.

And then history will mock you for a fool.

- Poor Dick Rowe at Decca Records in 1963 is alleged to have said, 'Guitar groups are on the way out,' as he turned down The Beatles.

- Ken Olsen, founder and chairman of DEC, went on record in 1977 to say, 'There is no reason anyone would want a computer in their home.'

- Daryl Zanuck, movie producer: 'Television won't last because people will soon get tired of staring at a plywood box every night.'

  Hollywood could have, should have piled into television early. But didn't. And came unstuck as a consequence.

- 'Children just aren't interested in witches and wizards any longer.' Unknown publisher writing to turn down J. F. K. Rowling's first *Harry Potter* manuscript.

- 'Rail travel at high speed is not possible because passengers, unable to breathe, would die of asphyxia.' Dr Dionysius Lardner, professor of natural history, 1823.

- Failing to spot the power of the invention, here's Henry Morton, president of the grandly named Institute of Technology, on the subject of Thomas Edison's electric lamp: 'Everyone acquainted with the subject will recognize it as a conspicuous failure.'

- 'The automobile is a novelty, only a fad.' The president of the Michigan Savings Bank in 1903 advising Henry Ford's lawyer not to invest in the company.

There are more.

- 'The world potential for copying machines is 5,000 at most.' IBM executives when rejecting the advances of the people who soon afterwards founded Xerox.

- 'This "telephone" has too many shortcomings to be seriously considered as a means of communication. The device is inherently of no value to us.' The anonymous writer of an internal memo at Western Union in 1876.

- 'There will never be a bigger plane built.' The engineer after the maiden flight of the Boeing 247, which accommodated as many as ten passengers.

Challenging assumptions is not easy.
It requires you to think the unthinkable.

Herman Kahn was lampooned as Dr Strangelove in Stanley Kubrick's film of the same name.

His misdemeanour was not just to plan for a nuclear war but to establish how America would win it.

Thinking the unthinkable is not asking who can put us out of business but what?

Kodak saw the threat from digital photography.

Heck, they invented it.

But what they did was to assume they could keep the lid on it by protecting the patents they owned.

It turned out they couldn't.

By contrast, Fujifilm did challenge assumptions.

By all accounts, they challenged every assumption they could think of.

One of the assumptions was that they were in the photography business.

Actually, what they were expert at was understanding antioxidants.

That expertise allowed them to make an unexpected detour from film to beauty products.

Ultraviolet light causes photographs to fade. It also causes skin to wrinkle and sag.

The technology that Fujifilm used to help their photos last longer also helps skin do the same.

Fuji launched Astalift in 2006, a cosmetics company, which, over the last ten years, has become a market leader in several countries.

There's a little parable that's told about how you cook a frog.

Drop it into boiling water and it will leap straight out.

Drop it into cold water and turn the heat up, then it will slowly cook to death.

That's the fate that befalls any business that ceases to examine what it does and why it does it regularly.

Think Kodak.

Be Fuji.

4. Imagine parallel worlds

Organizations have their own patterns.

Their processes have evolved over time to be as they are.

The way they budget, the way they scope, the way they do just about everything.

The problem here is that patterns ossify.

Then what happens is those organizations become resistant to change. Their procedures become slower and more byzantine than the competition's.

They get bogged down.

When Ford and Mazda merged, it is alleged that after some months it was decided that the marketing wings of the two companies in Europe should combine into one unit.

There were hundreds of people in the Ford marketing team.

The Mazda team had four people.

I suspect each team was equally stunned to learn of the other's size but that Ford found out more about themselves.

The way to break your own patterns is by looking at how other people do things and asking, if we were them, what would we do?

Obviously you don't want to copy them exactly, but getting into their mindset may help you see your own solution.

Within Google there is the mantra 'steal with pride'.

Ban, the first roll-on deodorant, was inspired by looking at Laszlo Biro's ballpoint pen, patented in 1943.

In one workshop I ran, a company that specialized in relocation services, helping employees of multinationals transfer from one part of the world to another, asked themselves, what would we do if we were Google.

'We'd skateboard around the office.'

Laughter.

'Brighten this place up a bit.'

Much agreement.

They hated their offices.

'We could be the civil service.'

It turned out that the offices were leased and the landlords would not tolerate any decoration at all.

But when the conversation turned towards the website, someone noted that they had no landlord here. Their site was their own.

They could be colourful, literally and metaphorically.

They could be really useful to their clients.

And have fun.

Ideas began to pour out of them. Like how they could make videos to help people explore their new cities, Street View experiences from their new offices of the cafes and bars nearby, bots that would answer questions.

I call this Parallel Worlds.

You set up the braindump as normal.

Describe the problem.

Describe what you want to achieve.

Then ask the group to name three organizations they admire.

When you have the three names down on the flipchart,

spend a few minutes on each remembering what it is those organizations do and do well.

If Doc Martens were facing the same challenge, what would they do?

If Facebook had these issues, what would Mark Zuckerberg do?

If Ron Dennis was in charge of this task force, what would he do?

Or, rephrased, what would you have to change about your company to be able to make eight innovations an hour?

If you were McDonald's, what would your equivalent of the Happy Meal be?

If you were Clark's shoes, how would you design the equivalent of your soles so they would leave a distinctive print behind?

If you were P. T. Barnum, what would your elephant be? (When Barnum's circus came to a new town, they announced their arrival by walking through the main street with Jumbo, their six-and-a-half ton elephant. Jumbo did more for sales than any number of posters.)

If ideas are oozing rather than flowing, get the group to start thinking about organizations that have very specific characteristics. For instance:

- Southwest Airlines. They put their employees first. Before their customers. 'We believe that if we treat our employees right, they will treat our customers right, and in turn that results in increased business and profits that make everyone happy.'

  In putting their employees first, they expect their employees to put their customers first. And they do.

  What about your company?

- Zappos' Tony Hsieh has abandoned all traditional management structures in favour of holacracy. This puts the onus on employees to manage themselves. Not everyone likes it. Eighteen per cent of Zappos' workforce took voluntary redundancy. But they were replaced rapidly with people happy to work in a less hierarchical structure.

    In the old-style system, you would have to ask for permission to bring your dog to work. A senior manager would (almost inevitably) say 'no'. In the new system you ask, if I bring my dog to work, does it make it unsafe for others? To which the idea is, probably not. So, even though he doesn't like dogs, Tony Hsieh is happy to have dogs on the premises. Well, he has to be.

    Incidentally, Zappos had a record year in terms of financial results.

So, in the braindump you can ask:

If we didn't need the approval of a manager (or managers), what would we do?

Would we accept responsibility? What would we do if it was our own money on the line?

How would we come to a decision? What would our decision look like?

- Dyson is said to invest about £1.5 million a week in R&D. If you invested as much, in which areas of research would you most want to spend your money?

    How would you turn innovation from a needs-must of the company to its very *raison d'être*?

Looking at your current issue, what would James Dyson do?

Remember, he built over 5,000 prototypes of his first cyclone cleaner, flirting with bankruptcy before he went to market.

Still, it did become the bestselling cleaner in Britain within twenty-three months.

- Chipotle's Steve Ells founded the fast-food chain around a single-minded proposition. Food with Integrity.

  All Chipotle ingredients are sourced from farmers who respect their animals and their acreage. Nothing from genetically modified stock. Nothing factory farmed. Nothing unethical.

  So, looking at your own problem, how could you solve it with ethics? What one thing could you do to make people admire what you represent?

  If you were to get behind a human value, what would it be?

  Unilever is restructuring itself around sustainability. Not so much because it makes them look like panda-cuddling nice guys but because it makes economic sense. Paul Polman believes global warming already costs the company €300 million a year.

You can also try:

Apple

FIFA

Harley Davidson

London Zoo

Nike

Rolex

Shakespeare

The Royal Family

5. Think the opposite

Paul Arden was the contrarian's contrarian.

He was the executive creative director of Saatchi & Saatchi when the agency was in its golden years.

When I first met him, he was at a less lustrous agency.

He wore T-shirts and jeans like the rest of us but when he went to work for the famous brothers, he transformed himself.

He did the opposite.

He became the only creative director to wear tailored suits.

Mind you, they weren't boring blue suits. But tweeds and Prince of Wales checks.

Despite coming from a relatively humble background he made himself look like an eccentric marquis.

In retirement, he wrote the book *Whatever You Think, Think the Opposite*. It was a follow-up to his massively successful *It's Not How Good You Are, It's How Good You Want to Be*.

'Start taking bad decisions and they will take you to places where others only dream of being.'

Some of his homilies are a touch glib.

In his defence, what he was trying to suggest is that most thinking processes are linear and logical.

If you encourage your mind to throw up the strange, the illogical or the downright contradictory, you open it up to new possibilities.

For instance, when Saatchi & Saatchi were briefed to come up with a campaign to promote the V&A Museum, the expected thing to do would have been to talk about the many fabulous collections or its claim to be the world's leading museum for art and design.

Instead, Arden persuaded them to buy the deliberately Cockney line, 'An ace caff with quite a nice museum attached.'

One of the stories he used to tell was of the Oxford don Maurice Bowra, who went swimming at Parson's Pleasure. This was a little patch of the River Cherwell, where nude bathing was allowed until 1991.

It just so happened that a punt full of young ladies went drifting by.

All the dons grabbed their towels to cover their bodies except for Bowra, who wrapped his towel around his head.

They covered their shame, he covered his identity.

Arden's general drift is that if you do the same as everybody else, then life will not only be dull but pointless.

So often doing it wrong turns out to be the right thing.

Steve Ells, founder of Chipotle, is on record as saying, 'So many people told me it was not a good idea to start a restaurant, especially a fast-food restaurant. There was so much wrong with it: it was too spicy; everything was done by hand, from scratch. Everything was wrong.'

When Wayne and Daryl Arnold decided in a Hong Kong bar that they would start a digital advertising agency, they too got it wrong.

They didn't realize that every other new agency was jettisoning media departments. WPP had just created stand-alone media independent Mindshare and the other networks were doing the same.

The fully integrated agency was toast.

It's just no one told Daryl and Wayne this and their agency offered media planning and buying from day one.

As it turned out, there were many clients thankful for all their campaign thinking under one roof rather than under two.

Now, twelve years after Profero, media departments are becoming agency must-haves once again.

Richard Rogers noticed that all buildings hid their ventilation and water pipes. So when he built the Pompidou Centre, he put them on the outside.

It made it easier to build the place but, more than that, made it astonishing to look at.

The way to structure this in a braindump is to ask:

- What happens if you reverse the usual order of things?

    It is usual to give workers a bonus after they have done the job, but one fruit farmer gave his pickers a bonus at the beginning of the season. He got better prices for his fruit because it had been picked more carefully.

- What happens if you do the opposite of what seems sane and logical?

    Inoculating people against cholera by infecting them with cholera would have seemed madness.

But Louis Pasteur invented the science of immunology when he did exactly that. The next step was to use snake poison to create an antidote for that same poison.

- What happens if your premise seems irrational?

    Scott Galloway is an unreasonable man.[49]

    He has told the story that when he got Series C funding for his first company, he asked for $30 million. His investors wanted to know what he proposed to do with this money.

    He told them he intended to take $17 million out for himself. These were unreasonable numbers, he agreed.

    His argument was, if he could get all the practicalities of life sorted, a place to live with no mortgage, his kids' education financed, then he could free his mind to concentrate on making the company not just more valuable but incredibly more valuable.

    He got the $30m.

- What happens if you do the opposite of what everyone else is doing?

    easyJet reversed the usual pricing structure of other airlines. Instead of selling the seats at full price then reducing the price the closer it got to the flight date, they charged more the closer it got to the flight. It seems to have worked. From two planes in 1995, easyJet now operates a fleet of 233.

    On the subject of airlines, Michael O'Leary is the famously controversial CEO of Ryanair. Where most airlines try to be polite to their passengers, he did the obverse. He was consistently rude about his customers. He gave press conferences to announce how he would be giving them less rather than more. This went as far as threatening to put coin-operated locks on the toilet doors of his planes, charging a pound to anyone who wanted to spend a penny.

Everything he did, though, underscored the proposition that Ryanair flights were the cheapest in Europe. All the add-ons were what cost the money.

- What happens if we insert the word 'not'?

Who do we *not* want using our product?

Most commercial directors of most companies assume that everybody is a potential customer. Renzo Rosso, by contrast, was very clear about who his target audience was not.

The founder of clothing empire Diesel saw how middle-aged men with paunches like me and Jeremy Clark were asphyxiating Levi's.

You can buy Levi's jeans with a 46-inch waist.

Frankly, my children would rather be found dead in the ditch than wear anything a saddo like me wears.

So Diesel jeans aren't available in anything larger than size 34 waist.

Diesel do not want me as a customer.

And I can understand why.

- Who would not want to buy our product or argument? Why do they not care? And does that insight bring a different perspective?

Leo Burnett Chicago created a brilliant campaign to keep Troy Public Library open when it looked certain to close. There was to be a public vote on the matter. To get book lovers involved and voting, small ads were created purporting to come from an anti-book lobby. 'Vote to close Troy Library – book burning party, 2 Aug!'

It worked. 12,246 people voted yes to save the library, 8,799 voted no.

- Remember 'Never let a good crisis go to waste'? It's a way of trying to look the other way down the telescope. There is a business opportunity to be had in almost every disaster.

   For instance, in 2008, when the Icelandic economy collapsed in the last week of September, a Danish entrepreneur was in Reykjavik in the first week of October buying their swanky 4×4s for a song.

- What can you tell people not to do? Tell people they can't do something and immediately they want to do it.

   When they do it, what do you do?

   Patagonia ran advertising that read: 'Don't buy this jacket'.

   They wanted people to think about consumerism. And, in the best interests of the planet, to buy their jackets only when they really needed to.

6. Make a wish

The word 'synectics' apparently means 'the tying together of seemingly unrelated elements'.

In 1970, George Prince wrote *The Practice of Creativity*, which detailed how he and his partner William Gordon worked in the company they established together, also called Synectics.

He wrote about metaphor thinking.

Creating images of things and looking for connections between what were apparently unrelated subjects led to innovations.

He was also incurably positive.

One of his techniques for kicking off a braindump was to float a crazy idea. The crazier the better.

Then everyone in the room had to talk about two things they liked about the idea.

What Synectics understood then and now is that emotion is dramatically important in generating ideas.

Fear, being one of the most powerful emotions of all, inhibits people.

Criticism, real or suggested, sends everyone in the room back into their shells.

So the set-up was designed to make everyone feel equally comfortable. Then they could come up with what they call 'springboard' ideas.

Another of their techniques is called 'Take a Walk'.

I've never used it but like the sound of it.

It's Edward de Bono meets Tony Buzan. Word and image forced into each other's company.

You select a key word.

Then leave the room.

Walk around the building, out into the street, looking for instances of your key word out there in the real world.

Then you try to bring what you have seen back to the problem.

Now, the Synectics people will probably hate me for this but at the heart of the Prince/Gordon methodology is wishful thinking.

Literally, to think about a problem and start a sentence relating to it with the words 'I wish . . .'

The great thing about wishes is that they turn you into Harry Potter.

A wish is a magic spell that allows anything to happen.

I wish I could make enough money to never have to work for that man *again.*

Or, *I wish there was an English fizzy drink.*

The story goes that when the team at Britvic were looking to extend Tango out into new flavours, they used synectics to help them.

Someone said, 'I wish that all fizzy drinks weren't so American.'

The build from that was, 'I wish we had a drink that was British in every bubble.'

The result was Blackcurrant Tango.

It was launched with a sampling exercise.

Here's the thought process they went through at the time.

Okay, we have a British fizzy drink. How do we launch it? What is so very British?

Answer: caravanning.

Only we Brits are eccentric enough to think spending a couple of weeks taking an aluminium box from one wet part of the country to another in the rain is enjoyable.

So, caravans.

What is very British and can pull the caravans?

Bentleys.

Mark C. was the young creative who came up with the idea of this most British of drinks being introduced to the public with this most British of cars.

In his twenties and in his jeans he went to the swanky car dealer on Berkeley Square.

He was eyeing up a particularly fine specimen of Bentleyness when he was approached by a salesman. In a suit.

'Can I help?'

'I'm just looking to see where I could fix a tow bar.'

'Bentleys don't have tow bars, sir.'

'Mine bloody will.'

Imagine it.

You're twenty-six years old and you go out to buy three Bentleys in an afternoon. That's what happens if you are a creative person.

You find solutions to business problems which project you into experiences you could never have imagined.

I wish parcels would deliver themselves.

Did someone from Amazon say something like this in a braindump?

Amazon drones look as if they may very well perform that service soon.

Elsewhere in the world of delivery, robots on wheels are already in test delivering pizzas in Manhattan.

I wish I didn't have to see animals in cages. It's upsetting.

I wish I could see them in something approaching their natural habitat.

And if you go to Animal Kingdom at Walt Disney World in Florida, your wish is granted.

In the story of how Animal Kingdom came about there is a wonderful example of a creative mind being applied to solve a very specific problem.

Whether the executive involved used any particular method or whether it was intuition we shall never know.

He had been working on the feasibility of Animal Kingdom for at least two years.

After the idea came clarification of what it would look like and how it might work.

What sort of animals? Where would they come from? How would they be safely exhibited?

Then evaluation. How much would it cost? How would those costs be recouped? What sort of pricing structure would be required?

A lot of work went into it.

He became convinced Animal Kingdom would be a huge success.

Finally, he got to present to the board of Disney.

In those days Michael Eisner was the chairman.

Among the non-execs was a gnarled street-fighter of a businessman.

He was not impressed by the concept of what was, in his view, a zoo by another name.

'Kids today aren't interested in animals. Have a look and see what they are watching online. What they do in their bedrooms. Animals are old hat. They're National Geographic, they are so lame.'

At this point, Mr Eisner had to close the meeting. It had run over time and board members had flights to catch.

'I'm sorry about this because we haven't reached an agreement.'

But he had a suggestion for the young exec.

'However, why don't you kick us off at the next board meeting in a month's time?'

Our hero's problem was that after years of work, he couldn't excite the board with his vision.

If he had been using synectics as an approach, he might have thought, *I wish I could get these guys as excited as I am about seeing wild animals up close and personal.*

Maybe he did use synectics. Because he had an idea.

At the next board meeting, when Animal Kingdom was the number one topic on the agenda, he walked into the room.

On a leash beside him he had a fully grown male Siberian tiger.

'Now, where were we? Ah, yes . . . animals are boring.'

He got the go-ahead.

7. Try scenario planning

This is when you ask the 'what if?' questions.

What if we are the victims of a massive fraud?

What if we double in size in the next year?

Funnily enough, sudden growth can be as damaging as a sudden shock, especially when you are a small business.

One computer games company I worked with had grown so fast, they had simply hired new bodies to throw at all the various issues.

Ten years later, it was an organizational shambles and haemorrhaging money unnecessarily.

Sometimes rapid growth can lead to cash flow problems.

What if there's a recession?

One bloke I knew was left some money in a will. So he used it to buy a chalet in the Swiss Alps so he could ski whenever he wanted.

He started renting it out.

His bank manager, noticing the money coming in, suggested he take out a loan to buy another chalet. And another.

Soon he had eight and business was good.

Then came recession and the bank that had been throwing money at him wanted it all back and he went bankrupt.

What if the boss gets divorced and his wife, a shareholder, holds the company to ransom?

I could write an entire book about the upheavals this has caused to a small family business I know.

What if the boss dies?

What if the boss goes to jail? One start-up I know of came tumbling down when their new business-savvy CEO turned out to be a crook.

What if your key people all leave?

Mike W., when he was managing the Ogilvy network across Europe, got an email one morning in which the entire staff of the Oslo office resigned. Every man jack of them. Taking, they thought, all the business with them.

These are micro-level questions and well worth a day's discussion with your key people.

Here are a few to help you get started.

— What if we lose our most important account?

— What if the landlord doubles our rent?

- What if we have a new competitor who does what we do cheaper and better? (I am reminded of the great Kenyan middle-distance runner Henry Rono, who was asked which of his competitors at the Kenyan national trials he feared most. 'The unknown person who just turns up without spikes,' he said. For many businesses, new competition is unexpected.)
- What if we get sued for some reason?
- What if we are subject to a PR disaster? (For instance, when two Domino's Pizza workers filmed themselves putting snot on the pizzas they were making, it took Domino's five days to respond.)
- What if our premises get burnt down?
- What if a larger company was to put in a bid to buy us?
- What if we win an award?
- What new product or product line can we develop?

As you talk about any scenario, if any of them was to unfold, try to discuss:

- What you ought to do
- What you should not do

At a macro level, it is extraordinary how very little scenario planning there seems to be.

Brexit.

Need I say more?

But going back in time a little, when the Allied forces piled into the Persian Gulf in August 1990 to deal with Saddam Hussein's invasion of Kuwait, they planned all the way up to the moment his troops retreated back inside their own borders.

Then nothing.

It's one of the reasons why the whole region is in such a state today.

Going back to 1973, wanting to give the West a bloody nose for their support of Israel in the Yom Kippur War, the oil-producing nations imposed an embargo on oil sales.

The price rocketed up from $2.50 to $11.00 a barrel, leading to an economic slump and soaring unemployment.

Thanks, guys.

Shell, however, had planned for just such an eventuality and were more agile in their response.

The Shell Scenarios division has been in place since the late 1960s and their work has allowed the company to anticipate several of the crises the world has faced, the collapse of apartheid and the AIDS epidemic among them.

They have been able to react to situations faster than their competitors and protect their business and their shareholders from meltdown.

BP may wish they had done something similar.

In fact, Shell has shared its more recent assessments of tomorrow's world in a section of their website called 'New Lenses on the Future'.

Before 11 September 2001, fewer than 40 per cent of American companies used scenario planning as a business tool. By 2006 that number had risen to 70 per cent.

The way to run a session of scenario planning is to start with a 'what if?'

Put people into groups of four.

The rules are: keep an open mind and keep it going. Play the game!

Ask each team to choose one of the big four: politics, the economy, technology or society. What big shifts can the group anticipate in each of those buckets?

You can have a fifth bucket, if you like. Call it 'Curved Balls' or something similar. What if an asteroid hits the planet? What if an epidemic on the scale of the Great Plague occurs?

The question to ask is what's *really* happening?

What's possible? What's plausible? What's probable? What's preferable?

What is the worst that could happen? What does the best possible outcome look like? Remember, what you are trying to do is come up with options, not with actions.

That said, do any of your options suggest decisions or actions you could be taking right now?

Encourage each team to present back by telling a story of how they imagine change and how they would respond to it.

What happens with stories is they gently nudge people's minds away from what they *know* to what they imagine.

The next phase is to sketch out the strategies you would have to have in place should any of those scenarios actually unfold.

It is a truism that all our knowledge is based on past experience but all our decisions are based on how we view the future.

What scenario planning does is force you to acknowledge that there is a lot you don't know. It may even remind you that there is even more that you don't know you don't know.

So, what can you do about it?

What practical steps can you take to fill in those gaps in your knowledge?

Scenario planning looks as if it is all about preparing your defences.

In fact, once you have run a session or two, you will see it is more about unlocking ideas about what you can be doing right now that will help you to adapt and evolve successfully.

8. Have yourself a hack

The hack is a relatively recent phenomenon, I think.

It is the braindump with added neurosis.

It looks to me rather like a 'kettling' technique for generating ideas.

It has become popular in the tech world and it seems to work.

The word was first used at MIT, where the students began organizing intense problem-solving events. Up until that moment, 'hacking' was what happened when you made your way illegally into the heart of someone else's data. Now it began to mean anything that was technologically clever. And that evolved into anything that solved a problem in an unusual way.

The way to organize a hack is to set a time – say 10 a.m. to 6 p.m. – and find a spacious location. You might need it because the idea is to get as many people as possible to come along. Put them into teams of four or five.

You brief them. Then let them go.

Because it's a hack, the intention is that they come up with ingenious ideas, unexpected ideas.

Because it's a hack, it is most likely to involve techies, people who can write code and who are immersed in technology.

Because it's a hack, they will usually try to build some sort of prototype to demonstrate how their ideas would work in practice.

It's competitive.

And deliberately pressured.

If you want more pressure, then turn the hack into a hackathon. Make it a twenty-four-hour session.

Make sure you have enough coffee or caffeine-packed drinks.

Open it to all and sundry.

If you're going to do this, though, make sure the purpose has some sort of social credibility to it.

In June 2013, Jon Oringer, CEO of Shutterstock, told the *New York Times* the company held regular internal hackathons.[50]

'A lot of people get really excited about them, and they can build whatever they want for the company – it could be crazy, practical, whatever. We actually wind up implementing a lot of those things. It's pretty amazing what people can get done in twenty-four hours.'

The theory is that hackathons work *because* of the pressure. *Because* the participants aren't able to escape.

Creative Social, a group of digital creative directors, organized a hack that was both literal and metaphorical.[51]

'Hack-a-Chuck' invited twenty of their tribe to do something, anything, amazing with a pair of Converse Chuck Taylor All-Star shoes.

As well as hacking metaphorically, i.e. coming up with innovative uses for the shoes, they also had to hack literally, carving them up to build their prototypes.

A pun, but a nice one.

At the end of the event, there were shoes that lit up when you walked, shoes that connected to an app on your smartphone to help you sharpen up your dance moves, shoes that became radios, shoes for guitar players with wah-wah pedals built in, shoes that direct you on interesting walks around the city with haptic widgets, shoes with pedometers, shoes that make graffiti and shoes that turn your movements into digital art.

Lastly, gloriously, one team who ignored tech completely and turned their shoe into a sculpture of a ship.

Personally, I am with James Webb Young on this, though. While working in a group can be a laugh, an idea always starts in one mind.

While hacks may be a good way to meet similar people and make new, interesting friends, you can't do better than give people who have ideas time to have the ideas.

CONCLUSION

Imagination is a unique human trait.

Creative people use the power of the imagination to project forward in time ideas about how things might work better.

Very occasionally, someone might have an idea which seems to have come from nowhere but which changes everything.

This is the act of invention.

Then what happens is other people start looking at the idea and working out how they can improve it and spin off from it. Turning their ideas into reality and putting a cost and a price against them is the act of innovation.

Since time immemorial, our species has looked at ways of making life easier, less terrifying and more rewarding.

We can't help having ideas.

The caveat here is that having ideas that will genuinely make a difference is not easy.

Education hasn't helped. Exams reward those who have learned parrot-fashion rather than those who start playing with their knowledge.

Yet creativity has never been so important.

For the individual, learning to have ideas and to express them is the way for personal growth.

Maslow was not alone in noticing that fulfilled people tend to be creative, in that they *do* stuff.

They don't sit in front of the telly.

They write, paint, carve, plant, design, tinker, mend. Creative people are *makers*.

Don't think about taking up an old interest or trying a new hobby. Do it.

Become a maker and you will change your life.

Really you will.

Similarly, it doesn't matter whether your business employs a couple of people or a couple of thousand.

If you can create space for the makers and do-ers, you will fashion a culture in which ideas keep popping up like spring flowers.

And then innovations in what you do, how you do it and even why you do it will become inevitable.

Incidentally, it will be enormous fun.

Bibliography

Paul Arden – *It's Not How Good You Are, It's How Good You Want to Be* (2003), Phaidon

Paul Arden – *Whatever You Think, Think the Opposite* (2006), Portfolio

Dave Brailsford – *21 Days to Glory* (2012), HarperCollins

Tony Buzan – *The Mind Map Book* (1996), Plume

Steve Chapman – *Can Scorpions Smoke?* (2014), Lulu.com

John Cleese – *So, Anyway* (2014), Random House Books

Mihály Csíkszentmihályi – *Creativity: The Psychology of Discovery and Invention* (1996), Harper Collins

Edward de Bono – *Lateral Thinking* (1970), Penguin

Edward de Bono – *Six Thinking Hats* (1985), Penguin

Sam Delaney – *Get Smashed* (2007), Sceptre

Peter Diamandis and Steven Kotler – *Abundance: The Future Is Better Than You Think* (2012), Free Press/Tantor Media

Charles Duhigg – 'What Google Learned From Its Quest to Build the Perfect Team' (16 February 2016), *New York Times Magazine*

James Dyson – *Against the Odds* (1997), Texere Publishing

Mark Earls – *Copy, Copy, Copy: How to Do Smarter Marketing by Using Other People's Ideas* (2015), John Wiley & Sons

Alex Ferguson – *Managing My Life* (1999), Hodder & Stoughton

Alex Ferguson – *Leading* (2015), Hodder & Stoughton

Timothy R. V. Foster – *101 Ways to Generate Great Ideas* (1991), Kogan Page

Louis V. Gerstner – *Who Says Elephants Can't Dance?* (2002),
Harper Business

Malcolm Gladwell – *Outliers* (2008), Little, Brown & Company

Malcolm Gladwell – 'The Creation Myth' (16 May 2011), *New Yorker*

Janet Gleeson – *The Arcanum* (1998), Warner Books

Seth Godin – *The Dip* (2007), Penguin Books

Noah J. Goldstein and Others – *Yes! 50 Secrets from the Science of Persuasion* (2007), Profile Books

Sir John Hegarty – *Turning Intelligence into Magic* (2011),
Thames and Hudson

Walter Isaacson – *Steve Jobs* (2011), Simon & Schuster

Rudyard Kipling – 'The Elephant's Child' (1902)

Jonah Lehrer – *Imagine: The Art and Science of Creativity* (2012),
Text Publishing

Bob Levenson – *Bill Bernbach's Book: A History of the Advertising That Changed the History of Advertising* (1987), Random House

Theodore Levitt – 'Marketing Myopia' (1960), *Harvard Business Review*

Gareth Lewis – *Successful Creativity in a Week* (1999), Hodder & Stoughton

David McCandless – *Information is Beautiful* (2009),
HarperCollins

Donald W. Mackinnon – 'The Nature and Nurture of Creative Talent' (1962), *American Psychologist*, Vol 17(7)

A. H. Maslow – 'A Theory of Human Motivation' (1943),
Psychological Review, Vol. 50

A. H. Maslow – *Motivation and Personality* (1954), Harper & Brothers

Jack V. Matson – *Innovate or Die* (1996), Paradigm Press

Alex Osborn – *Your Creative Power: How to Use Imagination* (1948), Scribner

Scott Plous – *The Psychology of Judgment and Decision Making* (1993), McGraw-Hill

George Prince – *The Practice of Creativity* (1970), Collier Books

Sir Ken Robinson – *Out of Our Minds* (revised 2011), Capstone

Bertrand Russell – *Principles of Social Reconstruction* (1916), Allen & Unwin

Eric Schmidt & Jonathan Rosenberg – *How Google Works* (2014), John Murray

Samuel Smiles – *Self Help* (1859), republished by General Books

Laurence Sterne – *The Life and Times of Tristram Shandy* (1759)

The Imagineers – *Walt Disney Imagineering* (1998), Hyperion

Edward E. Tufte – *Visual Explanations* (1986), Graphics Press USA

David Walsh – *Inside Team Sky* (2014), Simon & Schuster

James Webb Young – *A Technique for Producing Ideas* (1940, republished 1965. 2016 edition from Stellar Editions)

?WhatIf! – *Sticky Wisdom* (2002), Capstone

Clive Woodward – *Winning* (2004), Hodder & Stoughton

Acknowledgements

John Gordon is one of the most creative people I know. A serial entrepreneur, he produces startling ideas startlingly frequently. One of them was *Directory*, the magazine I now own and edit, and another is the how to: ACADEMY.

I am very grateful for the magazine, which has kept me in touch with innovations in technology and communications. And I'm grateful for the invitation to write this how-to book. It's something I just talked about for years until John called my bluff.

Thanks Frances for chivvying me along.

Thanks Martha for editing.

Thanks Steve Harrison for reading the first draft and being so helpful.

Thanks also to wife and best friend Dorte for her creativity in raising two remarkable children and for successfully bringing contemporary Scandi-cool to a seventeenth-century English barn.

Notes

1 *John Cleese on Creativity* – a training video on YouTube. youtube.com/watch?v=DMpdPrm6Ul4

2 If you are looking for an innovative accountant, go to acquisition-intl.com (The Voice of Corporate Finance), where you will find a list of the most innovative firms of the year.

3 Moore's Law: in 1965, Gordon Moore predicted that the processing power of computers of all sizes would double every two years thanks to the ability to double the number of transistors per square inch on their integrated circuit boards. It held true for fifty years and many believe it will hold true for twenty more.

4 For more on the American way of death, there is a book (which I haven't read), *Until You Are Dead: The Book of Executions in America* by Frederick Drimmer, 1992.

5 'Prey Preferences of the Leopard', *Journal of Zoology* (2006). zbs.bialowieza.pl/g2/pdf/1596.pdf

6 'The Big Won Rankings' – viewable at directnewideas. com/bigwon

7 *Guardian*, February 2015.

8 See Ron Dennis talking about competitiveness twenty-two minutes and thirty-seven seconds into youtube.com/watch?v=AYyN6zUgi-8

9 Mihály Csíkszentmihályi has written many books about the psychology of creative people, among them *Creativity:*

The Psychology of Discovery and Invention; *Flow: The Psychology of Happiness*; *Good Business: Leadership, Flow and the Making of Meaning*.

10 Study in Finland, 2013.

11 The Minnesota Center for Twin and Family Research continues its work to this day. Their website is: mctfr. psych.umn.edu/research/UM%20research.html

12 Sir Ken Robinson's TED talk: youtube.com/ watch?v=iG9CE55wbtY. But see also his talk at the RSA, 'Changing Education Paradigms': thersa.org/discover/ videos/rsa-animate/2010/10/rsa-animate---changing-paradigms

13 Gerstner describes the turnaround of IBM in his book *Who Says Elephants Can't Dance?*

14 Maslow's 'Hierarchy of Needs' was first given an airing in *Psychological Review* in 1943. He developed his thinking and in 1954 published *Motivation and Personality*. That evolved into the 1962 book *Toward a Psychology of Being*.

15 'The Creation Myth' was originally published in the *New Yorker* magazine, May 2011. newyorker.com/ magazine/2011/05/16/creation-myth

16 Sam Delaney's book *Get Smashed*, about the great advertising of the sixties, seventies and eighties, pays tribute to John in its title. His 'Martians' commercial for Cadbury's Smash was regularly voted as Britain's favourite TV ad.

17 Charles Handy started writing about business issues but slowly migrated towards ethics and philosophy. His books are speculative and thoughtful rather than filled with charts and diagrams (apart from the Sigmoid Curve!).

18 In addition to *John Cleese on Creativity* (video from a training) posted by AuthenticEducation: youtube.com/

watch?v=DMpdPrm6Ul4, see also *John Cleese on Creativity* posted by Any-idea? Collective: youtube.com/watch?v=5xPvvPTQaMI and *So, Anyway*, published by Talks at Google: youtube.com/watch?v=2-p44-9S4O0

19 Jonah Lehrer was a Rhodes Scholar, who wrote a series of books about creativity, linking the humanities and science, dare I say it, artfully. *How Creativity Works*, published in 2012, got him into hot water when it was alleged he had recycled a lot of his own work, plagiarized from others and fabricated chunks of it. Clearly it doesn't pay to be too creative when you write about creativity. Note to self.

20 May I recommend The Cloud Appreciation Society to you? If you can't get to look at clouds in your back garden, you see lots of them on their joyous website cloudappreciationsociety.org

21 Gary Dahl was also a copywriter and adman. In 2007 he published *Advertising for Dummies*, which did not make him nearly as much money as his pet rock.

22 Duke Ellington wrote over a thousand pieces of music, of which 'Soda Fountain Rag' was the very first.

23 Graham Fink's exhibition 'Nomads' is described, and several of his images shown, in this blogpost: creativebrief.com/blog/2014/01/13/fink%E2%80%99s-faces-making-the-crossover-from-advertising-into-art/

24 Uploaded by FORA.tv: youtube.com/watch?v=CsGihiSE6sM

25 Woburn Walk described: londonunveiled.com/2013/07/04/woburn-walk/

26 !WhatIf?, *Sticky Wisdom* p.41.

27 There is a short excerpt from Jung's book *Man and His Symbols* about synchronicity read aloud on YouTube,

uploaded by Jungian Maps: youtube.com/watch?v=BX_
nMwYa-nw

28 Conversely, BBC Focus polled readers of the *Radio Times*
on the *worst* ideas ever.

   1 – Weapons. 2 – Mobile phones. 3 – Nuclear power.
   4 – The Sinclair C5. 5 – Television. 6 – The car.
   7 – Cigarettes. 8 – Fast food. 9 – Speed cameras.
   10 – Religion.

29 *Daily Telegraph*, 23 June 2015.

30 *Fortune* magazine published an article entitled
'Why Snapchat Might Actually Be Worth $20 billion' on
26 May 2016: fortune.com/2016/05/26/snapchat-worth-
20-billion/

31 Source: UN report of 29 July2015: un.org/en/
development/desa/news/population/2015-report.html

32 The Gunn Report was founded by Donald Gunn in 1999
and is an annual measure of creative excellence in the
advertising industry: gunnreport.com

33 Elmwood website: elmwood.com/

34 Entrepreneur.com has a short video of her explaining her
system at: entrepreneur.com/video/238224

35 The *HBR* article is online at: hbr.org/2000/07/waking-up-
ibm-how-a-gang-of-unlikely-rebels-transformed-big-blue

36 nytimes.com/2016/02/28/magazine/what-google-
learned-from-its-quest-to-build-the-perfect-team.html?_
r=0

37 pechakucha.org/

38 As well as writing *A Technique for Producing Ideas*,
James Webb Young turned agency J. Walter Thompson
into an international network. He also helped created
the Advertising Council, today generating more public
interest messages than any other organization in the USA.

39 *Directory* is available online as well as offline, at: directnewideas.com

40 As well as many novels, of which perhaps *Myra Breckenbridge* is the best known, Gore Vidal was also credited as a scriptwriter on *Ben Hur*.

41 Other books from Mark Earls include *Welcome to the Creative Age* (2002) and *Herd: How To Change Mass Behaviour* (2007).

42 Malcolm Gladwell, 'The Creation Myth', *New Yorker*, May 2011.

43 Sir Frank Lowe was the young and charismatic MD of agency CDP, a creative hotshop in the sixties and seventies. He then founded Lowe Howard-Spink, which morphed into Lowe & Partners Worldwide when he sold the company to Interpublic Group in 1990. He was knighted in 2002 for services to advertising.

44 'The Invisible Japanese Gentlemen' (1965). You can read it online at the *Spectator* Archive: archive.spectator.co.uk/ article/7th-january-1966/9/short-story.

45 On Friday 13 August 2010 Simon Rogers wrote about Florence Nightingale's visualization of data in the *Guardian*: theguardian.com/news/datablog/2010/ aug/13/florence-nightingale-graphics

46 David McCandless on YouTube: youtube.com/ watch?v=5Zg-C8AAIGg. See also his website, informationisbeautiful.net/, and his books, *Knowledge is Beautiful, Information is Beautiful, The Visual Miscellaneum*, etc.

47 'The Elephant's Child' is one of the 'Just So' stories written and illustrated by Rudyard Kipling. It was published in 1902.

48 *Principles of Social Reconstruction* (1916).

49 Scott Galloway is professor of marketing at NYU Stern
School of Business and a successful content creator. His
YouTube channel, L2inc, has over 50,000 subscribers and
his video *The Four Riders of the Apocalypse* has had over
one million views. Not bad for a video about business.

50 nytimes.com/2013/06/21/business/jon-oringer-of-
shutterstock-on-the-power-of-the-hackathon.html

51 Creative Social was founded by Daniele Fiandaca and
Mark Chalmers. They organize events and publish books
such as *Hacker, Maker, Teacher, Thief*. creativesocial.com

Index

Page references styled in *italics* indicate
illustrations.